D0358255

Mary Berry is known to millions through her cookery spot on Thames Television's magazine programme, *Afternoon Plus*. She is a regular contributor to BBC *Woman's Hour* and often takes part in BBC and local radio phone-in programmes.

Mary Berry is known for her cookery writing in such magazines as *Ideal Home*, *Home and Freezer Digest* and *Family Circle*. She is one of Britain's most popular cookery writers, and has written more than twenty cookery books.

Also by Mary Berry in Sphere Books:

FAST CAKES
MORE FAST CAKES
CHOCOLATE DELIGHTS
FEED YOUR FAMILY THE HEALTHIER WAY
FRUIT FARE
FAST STARTERS, SOUPS AND SALADS
FAST SUPPERS
FAST DESSERTS

BUFFETS

Mary Berry

SPHERE BOOKS LIMITED

SPHERE BOOKS LTD
Published by the Penguin Group
27 Wrights Lane, London W8 5TZ, England
Viking Penguin Inc., 40 West 23rd Street, New York, New York 10010, USA
Penguin Books Australia Ltd, Ringwood, Victoria, Australia
Penguin Books Canada Ltd, 2801 John Street, Markham, Ontario, Canada L3R 1B4
Penguin Books (NZ) Ltd, 182–190 Wairau Road, Auckland 10, New Zealand

Penguin Books Ltd, Registered Offices: Harmondsworth, Middlesex, England

First published in Great Britain 1986 by Judy Piatkus (Publishers) Ltd
Published by Sphere Books Ltd 1988

Copyright © Mary Berry, 1986
All rights reserved

Made and printed in Great Britain by
Richard Clay Ltd, Bungay, Suffolk

Except in the United States of America,
this book is sold subject to the condition
that it shall not, by way of trade or otherwise,
be lent, re-sold, hired out, or otherwise circulated
without the publisher's prior consent in any form of
binding or cover other than that in which it is
published and without a similar condition
including this condition being imposed
on the subsequent purchaser

CONTENTS

INTRODUCTION

Before I began writing this book I thought it a good idea to get out the dictionary and check that a buffet did actually mean a help-yourself meal. The word was originally applied to an item of furniture, but gradually evolved to become, to quote, 'a sideboard or refreshment bar for the service of food where guests help themselves'. Which is exactly right, and for me a buffet is one of the most practical and enjoyable ways of entertaining friends for a meal.

A buffet can be as formal or informal as you like; it can be inside or outside; the food can be hot or cold, depending on taste or, more pertinent perhaps, on the season; and so much can be prepared in advance. With food arranged on a buffet table and the guests happily helping themselves, the host or hostess is very much more free to relax, move among the guests and have a good time as well. Buffet parties are thus a very great favourite of mine!

THE INVITATIONS

I find it best to give about six weeks' notice, especially around busy times like Christmas. It is a help for guests not only to know the date, time and place of the party, but also what to wear. I'm always delighted when I'm given written or verbal advice such as 'Informal please, John won't be wearing a tie as we plan to eat in the garden' or 'I want this to be a special party. I will be wearing my new long skirt, so please keep me company.' Written invitations for bigger parties are advisable and clearer, but do remember the RSVP bit, otherwise it can get out of hand! If you ask friends well ahead by telephone, it is a good idea to give a reminder a couple of days beforehand. This, I might say, is from experience. I well remember spending a Saturday evening at home, eating a simple omelette with Paul, and then opening my diary the next day to see that we should have been at a very special party the night before. Thank goodness they were dear friends and forgave me when I rang straightaway to explain!

THE MENU
AND THE RECIPES

The recipes that follow are mostly for twelve, a number that is easy to halve or double for parties. Start by choosing your occasion – a French or Danish buffet, if you want to follow my international ideas – and then the main dish. After this you can work the other courses around it. One of the next most important considerations is seating. If you are single-handed, it is best to prepare no more than one hot course. The guests may help themselves, but they'll want to sit down to eat; if you can't seat them all and some have to stand up to eat, choose food that can be tackled with a fork or a spoon.

Choose a menu that takes advantage of foods in season. It is crazy to go to great lengths to produce an exotic fruit salad of expensive tropical fruits in the height of midsummer; this is the time when home-grown strawberries and raspberries are at their peak, very reasonably priced and quite delicious.

When planning the menu, choose some dishes that can be made and frozen well ahead, and some items that can be made a day or two ahead and kept in the refrigerator. I always use a large pad of foolscap paper and make myself a simple countdown for at least the week beforehand. If I don't, I find myself going into town one day to collect the dry cleaning, next day to get general shopping, and later out to the trout farm. With more careful organisation one trip would have done it and I could have frozen the trout in the freezer for a few days. Each of the suggested menus throughout the book has a general work plan and time schedule which will help.

Make sure that the meal is a balanced one. Obviously, it must not have cream in every course, and a fish starter should not be followed by salmon! If you are making a quiche for the starter or main course, then naturally you wouldn't serve a flan, again with pastry, for pudding. A fruit or creamy pudding would be better. Choose dishes that are a contrast in colour and texture too.

First Courses

It is not always necessary to serve a first course at a buffet. It is sometimes a good idea to go straight into the main course, ensuring that there is plenty of room left for a special pudding! However, there are occasions when a first course is expected, particularly if your buffet party is in celebration of something very special.

I think buffet first courses should be as simple as possible – preferably cold – especially when catering for a crowd. And do try to have them already prepared on individual plates wherever possible. This makes serving so much easier. There is a time and place for everything of course; a warming bowl of soup on a chilly day would be welcomed, particularly if you are serving cold meats and salads as the main course; a mug of steaming soup would be even more appreciated during or after a firework display on a cold November night!

Puddings

No meal is really complete without a pudding and, as it's not every day that you entertain, you can go to town on this final course and give your guests something to remember! Choose one that will complement the rest of the meal; something light after a filling main course, something more substantial after a lighter dish. (Avoid cream if you have served it in other courses.) In fact, I like to offer a choice of puddings, cheese and biscuits and perhaps fresh fruit – it is surprising how many people really prefer an apple or a few grapes at the end of a meal.

Wherever possible, I find it a good idea to prepare the puddings in individual serving dishes so guests can easily help themselves; it also ensures that there is plenty to go round and that nobody is getting a bigger helping than anybody else. Ramekin dishes are ideal for fools, mousses and icecreams, and they look good too. Puddings such as flans, pies and tarts can be left in the tin, or turned out on to a plate and marked into wedges to make for easier serving. Decorate puddings flamboyantly: heads of fresh flowers – small roses or camellias – and leaves around a dish look beautiful. Cheese looks good arranged on vine or blackcurrant leaves.

Most of the puddings throughout the book can be prepared at least a day ahead and kept in the refrigerator until required; in some cases, this actually improves them as the flavours are given a chance to develop and creams time to chill. Most importantly, it gives you the chance to relax a little, knowing that you don't have to worry about the pudding on the day of the party!

KEEPINGS THINGS HOT OR COLD

Both can be a problem if you're catering for large numbers. A coolish oven is obviously the best place for foods to be served hot; a bain-marie on top of the stove can deal with accompaniments – several dishes or pans in one roasting tin of hot water over gentle heat. If the oven is full, where do you heat the plates? You can soak them in hot water (but you need to waste time drying them) or you can put them through the drying process or a short wash and dry in a dishwasher. Remember that it takes considerably longer to heat a pile of plates than just six. Start heating them a couple of hours ahead on a gentle heat in a hot cupboard, or in a second oven if you have one (and there's space) so that they are really hot but not too hot to handle. Swap the plates around so they are evenly heated.

When serving cold foods, decide first of all what dishes do not really need to be in the fridge. Salad ingredients keep well in a large lidded saucepan or casserole dish in a cold place (the larder, perhaps, or the floor of a north-facing garage or outhouse). It is essential for meat, fish and most cooked dishes to be kept in the refrigerator until shortly before the party, so you could perhaps ask to borrow some space in a good neighbour's fridge!

To keep a large quantity of wine chilled, make lots of ice cubes and ice blocks in old clean icecream containers in the freezer. Start doing this several days before and keep emptying them out into polythene bags to re-store in the freezer. Put the blocks and cubes in a clean plastic baby's bath, bucket or even a clean dustbin just before the party, and store most of the wine there. A few bottles can be stored in the fridge if there's room.

THE BUFFET TABLE

The table or tables for buffet parties needn't be of wonderful quality. If you have a splendid large dining table, fine (but do protect it adequately); if not, anything can be used, as the table will be covered completely by a cloth. Sturdy side tables or card tables can be placed together; even trestle tables or a wall-papering table can do, either inside or, preferably, in the garden. Never worry if tables are not the same size if you are joining them together for a buffet; the main consideration is that they are the same height. When covered with a cloth, all is hidden from sight (before they are laid, most restaurant tables are very tatty underneath!). But if you are using a really good polished dining table or sideboard, do put heatproof mats or something on it under the tablecloth or runner to stop it being stained by heat or liquid. A heavy blanket, even layers of newspaper, under the cloth, will often do the trick.

It is fun to go to town on a colour scheme for the table, relating it to the 'nationality' of the party. Old cotton sheets can be dyed and used as table-cloths, and I've done this very satisfactorily in the washing machine. One practical way of protecting the table and making it look good at the same time is to cover it to the floor with a colourful patterned or plain polyester and cotton sheet then top it with a plain or patterned plasticised cotton shiny or matt piece of material (bought by the yard from some good department stores). Choose the two fabrics to complement each other. Leave just enough of the top layer to hang 2–3 inches (5–7.5 cm) over the top of the table surface, and the bottom sheet then hangs down below like a skirt. Spills can be easily mopped up from the table. For a pretty Victorian effect, put a lacy cloth over a contrasting cloth or sheet.

For big parties, you might want to invest in a giant roll of paper tablecloth fabric. It comes in various colours and qualities, and the best looks and feels like felt. It is available from many good department stores.

If the buffet table has a plain cloth, a swagging of another fabric, greenery, flowers or ribbons looks lovely. Swagging is flounces of material or a chosen item pinned in at intervals along the visible edges of the table (all round, of course, if the table can be approached from all sides). This treatment is perhaps only applicable when you're using old tables: pins in the best Sheraton isn't a good idea! One of the most effective swaggings is trails of green Smylax, which can be ordered from a flower shop or flower accessory shop: it is expensive but wonderful for a wedding or something very special, particularly with a plain white cloth. Trailing ivy, real or artificial, looks good, or you could use evergreen and variegated leaves which you can wire on rope or sturdy string. Ask help with this from any keen flower-arranging friends. Posies of flowers look pretty at intervals, too, but they can get knocked off.

Match your general colour scheme and cloth with paper napkins, which come in various colours, sizes, patterns and qualities. I find it safest to keep to plain ones, except for Christmas parties. Candles make a buffet table special, but do make sure they are long enough to last the evening, and that they're in a safe place: they might get knocked over if people lean across to get at a particular dish. All these items can be ordered or bought well ahead of time to give you peace of mind. Flowers look lovely on a buffet table, but they too could get knocked over – and they tend to take up valuable table space! (Arrange them elsewhere.)

ARRANGING THE BUFFET TABLE

This needs forethought. Arrange the serving table or tables logically, so that the guests start by collecting a plate then take the food and lastly pick up the cutlery and a drink (although the bar should, preferably, be elsewhere). This means, therefore, that plates are piled at the nearest end of the table. Arrange the starter dishes next if you're having one, then the main course, vegetables or salads, and lastly the sauces, garlic bread, condiments, etc. Here, too, you want the cutlery and napkins. Have plenty of large serving spoons for vegetables and puddings, and ladles for soups and casseroles.

For every fifty guests, allow a separate serving table, otherwise the party can turn into just one long queue! If possible, have a separate table for the puddings and coffee, which could be arranged while the main course is being served. While the puddings are being served the main table could be used to deposit empty dishes and plates, which should be whisked away out of sight for washing up. Have somebody helping with that chore: there's nothing more enervating for a hostess – or guest – than a pile of dirty dishes. Hide them away, well scraped, in a corner, in a cupboard, in the dishwasher, or outside the back door! Have jugs of warm soapy water standing beside the sink for the cutlery to soak in, handles up.

SERVING THE FOOD

I usually arrange for the main dish to be served by me or a helper, and then the guests help themselves to all the other items.

Arrange most savoury dishes on or in fairly shallow dishes; the exception is stew or casseroles which can be served much more easily with a ladle from their deeper dish. (Have a practice beforehand and see how much a ladleful of casserole will serve; a portion is usually two small ladlefuls or one large.)

If there are twenty-four guests, say, I find it best to do two separate dishes for twelve, which means that the dish doesn't start to look too messy or pathetic towards the end! If the dish is for twelve, put twelve decorative garnishes on top – sprigs of parsley, watercress or dill, perhaps, or wedges of lemon: this not only looks good but can help whoever is serving to work out the correct portions. If the main dish is being served by a helper, you or someone else can arrange croûtons or other garnishes on each plate as it is served.

Let guests help themselves to individual puddings, cheese and coffee, making sure that everything they will need is nearby.

HIRING EQUIPMENT AND CHINA

For a large party, it is often necessary to hire and there are many sources. Go by personal recommendation if you can, but otherwise check your local paper or Yellow Pages. I recently hired some very pretty china at 5 pence per item, delivered in sensible washing-up bowls, labelled and covered with clingfilm. This was then collected dirty and the company washed it and stacked it again in washing-up bowls ready for the next hiring. All very easy and efficient, and *so* timesaving (the washing-up is the only thing I dislike about larger parties).

If you have a lot of parties, you could invest in some inexpensive seconds of china, as I have done and which will prove cheaper than hiring in the long run. You can buy seconds from the principal manufacturers who sometimes have seconds shops or factory warehouses. Department-store sales will have a good selection too. Choose a plain colour or simple design – the *food* should be the picture on the plate – but remember, of course, that you will need storage space!

RECIPE SERVINGS

Unless otherwise stated, the recipes in this book serve 12 people and can easily be multiplied to serve larger numbers.

Sample menus are based on the amounts given in the recipes. If this quantity has been increased, to serve a larger number of people, this is indicated in the menu.

FINGER FOODS

Finger foods can be very small, as often they're just nibbles to go with drinks. But if you know that your guests are the hungry kind, make them larger! It is difficult to say how many items people are going to eat as it all depends on the time of day and how near it is to their last meal. As a general rule, I allow between five and six items per person, plus the usual nuts, crisps, etc. This Christmas I gave a drinks party for 120 people: I made 1,000 *very* tiny eats and they all went! People were hungry at 6.30 pm that Saturday evening as most of them hadn't had much lunch (they were out Christmas shopping). The Christmas eating binge hadn't properly started, so it was all new! However, as Christmas parties went on I noticed that everyone was eating much less. I discussed this with a well-known London caterer: he said he allowed about eight eats per head, according to size.

For a wedding finger-food buffet, the eats need to be larger and more substantial. As this is often considered to take the place of lunch it is wise to allow eight to ten items per person. For larger numbers allow about 10 per cent *less* pro rata as, for some unknown reason, it works out that more people eat less!

Very fresh small smoked salmon sandwiches are a simple special addition. These look good arranged in rows with lemon wedges and cress or parsley. Also include some hot grilled or fried cocktail sausages. These can be cooked ahead and reheated then spiked with wooden cocktail sticks. If liked, they can be served with a Barbecue Sauce (page 177) for dunking.

Puddings are seldom considered at a finger-food party, but it's nice to finish off with something sweet. I've included recipes for two sweet mouthfuls which would make a delicious ending to any sort of buffet meal.

Drinks are difficult to advise on. Usually at a cocktail party, you are offered gin and tonic, whisky and soda or whatever you desire. This will be very time-consuming if you have to prepare individual drinks for large numbers, unless you have (or hire) someone to help. (Make sure this helper knows his stuff: at one party I heard about, a hired waiter didn't know a Manhattan from a Harvey Wallbanger, and there were some curious concoctions appearing in people's hands!) Wine or Bucks Fizz or something similar which can be served from a jug would be much easier. A mulled wine is easy too, for a Christmas celebration, as it's warming and can be prepared in advance.

Menu

DRINKS PARTY FOR 50

1lb (450g) Home-Fried Nuts

2 × Avocado Dip

2 × Baby Tomatoes with Cream Cheese

3 × Fishy Boats

100 Hot grilled baby sausages

2 × Hot Barbecue Sauce
(page 177)

2 × Cheese Almond Biscuits

Preparations Hints

This total menu can be prepared the day ahead of the party.
Only the boats and the tomatoes need filling on the day.

Home-Fried Nuts

Almonds are my favourite. If liked, a little sunflower oil can be added to the butter to lighten it. These can be fried a couple of days ahead. It's *essential* to drain every scrap of fat from the nuts.

Avocado Dip

Make the day before. Cover with clingfilm to touch the top of the dip to prevent discoloration. The vegetables for dipping can be prepared a day ahead and kept in the fridge in a polythene box.

Baby Tomatoes with Cream Cheese

These 'Gardener's Delight' tomatoes just need to be cut in half and seeds removed the day before; the cheese mixture can be piped on top on the day. You may need to dab each tomato half dry with kitchen paper to get the filling to stay in the shell.

Fishy Boats

Bake the pastry cases a day ahead, cool then store in a tin. On the day fill with the chosen freshly made-up fishy filling.

Sausages and Sauce

Cook both these the day before, store in the fridge, then reheat on the day.

Cheese and Almond Biscuits

Make a week or so ahead if this fits in with your timing. They should be kept in an air tight tin then refreshed if need be in a moderate oven for about 10 minutes.

Menu

CHRISTMAS PARTY FOR 12

Glühwein
(page 179)

2 × Cheese Filo Puffs

Sardine-Stuffed Eggs

2 × Melon and Parma Ham

Mini Pissaladières

Avocado Dip

Preparations Hints

This shouldn't prove too much bother in the midst of all your Christmas preparations, and most can be made a day or two in advance.

Glühwein

Make it the day before – in whatever quantities you deem necessary! – and leave to cool overnight. The next day strain out the spices and lemon rind, reheat until piping hot before your guests arrive. Any left over can be bottled, kept in the fridge, then reheated on the next cold Saturday or Sunday morning perhaps!

Cheese Filo Puffs

Can be made ahead, well wrapped and frozen, then thawed overnight and baked as needed.

Sardine-Stuffed Eggs

Boil the eggs the day before, and make the filling. Keep covered separately in the fridge. Assemble on the day.

Melon and Parma Ham

Quick to make on the day.

Mini Pissaladières

Best on the day, but can be made a day or two ahead. Reheat as needed and serve hot.

Menu

WEDDING BUFFET FOR 50

2 × Cheese Aigrettes

4 × Hot Prawn Vol-au-Vents

3 × Melon and Parma Ham

3 × Bacon and Liver Kebabs

2 × Asparagus Rolls

150 Hot Grilled Baby Sausages

3 × Hot Barbecue Sauce
(page 177)

2 × Brown Sugar Meringues

3 × Baby Chocolate Eclairs

Preparation Hints

There is a good balance of savouries here. Supplement, if liked, with tiny smoked salmon sandwiches in brown bread, and decorate dishes with cress and lemon wedges.

Cheese Aigrettes

Make either a day ahead or up to a couple of weeks ahead and freeze. Thaw, then reheat just before serving.

Hot Prawn Vol-au-Vents

Bake the vol-au-vent cases a day or two ahead, and store carefully. Make the prawn filling on the day, fill the cases and reheat.

Bacon and Liver Kebabs

Cook and cool a couple of days ahead, refrigerate, then reheat uncovered when needed.

Asparagus Rolls

Make a day ahead. Pile neatly on the serving dish, cover tightly with clingfilm, and chill until ready to serve.

Sausages and Sauce

Cook both a day ahead. Store in the fridge then reheat.

Brown Sugar Meringues

Make up to a couple of weeks ahead. Store in tins or sealed poly bags. Sandwich with cream on the day.

Chocolate Eclairs

Make the choux pastry eclairs up to three weeks ahead, then cool and freeze. Thaw, then crisp up in the oven, cool, fill with cream, and ice them on the day. The icing could be made a day ahead and reheated before dipping the eclairs.

Avocado Dip

Place the bowl of dip in the middle of a large platter and surround with pre-pared crisp vegetables such as cauliflower florets, sticks of celery, cucumber and carrot, small button mushrooms, radishes, broccoli spears and chicory leaves.

Cut the avocados in half and remove the stones. Scoop the flesh from the skin, and put it in a processor or blender with all the remaining ingredients. Process until smooth, taste and check seasoning, then turn into a bowl.

4 ripe avocado pears
6 oz (175g) rich cream cheese
juice of 1 large lemon
1 very small onion, grated
salt
freshly ground black pepper

Garlic Cheese Dip

Serve the dip in a bowl surrounded by a variety of fresh crisp vegetables and potato crisps or cheese straws.

Soften the cheese in a bowl with a wooden spoon then blend in the cream, garlic, chives and seasoning. Turn into a bowl and chill in the refrigerator for several hours before serving to give the flavours a chance to develop.

1lb (450g) rich cream cheese
½ pint (300 ml) soured cream
4 fat cloves of garlic, crushed
2 tablespoons snipped chives
salt
freshly ground black pepper

Baby Tomatoes with Cream Cheese

These tiny sweet tomatoes make a refreshing base for savouries to serve on a buffet table. The smallest ones can be speared on a cocktail stick with a cube of ham or cheese and eaten in one mouthful.

Scoop out and discard the seeds from the tomatoes with a small pointed teaspoon. Mix the cheese with a little milk or single cream until soft and smooth. Fill a piping bag fitted with a small rose piping tube with the softened cheese, and pipe a swirl of cheese inside each tomato shell.

Arrange on a platter and sprinkle with a little freshly chopped parsley just before serving.

about 20 cherry tomatoes, halved
4oz (100g) full-fat cheese with garlic and parsley
a little single cream or top of the milk
a little freshly chopped parsley, to decorate

Makes 40 tiny savouries

Melon and Parma Ham

1 small melon
6 thin long slices of Parma ham
juice of ½ lemon
freshly ground black pepper
lemon wedges, to garnish

Parma ham can now be bought in vacuum packs from most good supermarkets. When buying the melon, choose whatever is the best for the time of the year, and be sure it will be ripe for when you want to serve it.

Cut the melon into eight wedges. Scoop out and discard the seeds from each slice and cut off the skin. Divide the wedges into mouthful-sized pieces. Roll an appropriately sized piece of ham around each chunk of melon, and spear with a cocktail stick to make for easier eating.

Arrange the melon on a platter and squeeze the lemon juice over it. Season with a little black pepper and decorate with lemon wedges.

Serve well chilled.

Makes about 30

Asparagus Rolls

1lb (450g) frozen asparagus
 spears, thawed
1 small Hovis loaf
4oz (100g) butter, softened

It is essential to use a Hovis loaf when making asparagus rolls as this is the easiest bread to roll without it all crumbling and breaking up.

Blanch the asparagus in a pan of boiling salted water for a minute, then refresh under running cold water and drain well on kitchen paper. Cut the crusts off the loaf so that the loaf measures 2½ inches (6cm) square, then carefully slice the loaf into slices (you should get about thirty-six) with a very sharp bread knife. Butter the slices of bread and lay a spear of asparagus diagonally across the piece of bread from corner to corner.

Carefully roll up the bread so there is a V-shape on top of the roll.

Arrange on a serving dish, cover with clingfilm and store in the refrigerator until required.

Makes about 36

Bacon and Liver Kebabs

These tiny kebabs can be prepared well in advance and refrigerated, and then arranged on a serving dish and reheated in the oven as required.

Rinse any blood from the livers, dry on kitchen paper then toss in the seasoned flour until evenly coated. Heat the oil in a pan and quickly fry the livers for about 2 minutes until just tender. Remove from the heat, drain well on kitchen paper, and cut each in half. Wrap each of the livers in a piece of bacon, pierce with a wooden cocktail stick and cook under a hot grill until the bacon is crisp. Allow to cool then arrange on a heatproof serving dish ready to heat through when required.

To serve, cook in the oven at 350°F/180°C/Gas Mark 4 for about 25 minutes until warmed through.

Makes about 12

8oz (225g) chicken livers
2oz (50g) seasoned flour
sunflower oil, for frying
6 rashers of streaky bacon, cut in half

Cheese Aigrettes

These little savoury choux pastry balls are good to serve as a snack with drinks. Alternatively, serve at the end of a meal with coffee rather than a mint chocolate. When I had a Victorian buffet party to celebrate my birthday, I served them right at the end of the meal as a course in their own right.

Put the butter and water in a small pan and bring to the boil. Remove from the heat and add the flour all at once. Beat well until the mixture is smooth and glossy and leaves the sides of the pan clean. Cool slightly. Lightly mix the yolks and eggs together and beat into the mixture a little at a time. Stir in the cheese and seasoning.

Drop the mixture in teaspoonfuls into hot deep fat and fry gently until golden brown. Lift out and drain on kitchen paper. Serve warm.

To reheat the aigrettes for a party, arrange them on a baking sheet and heat in the oven at 425°F/220°C/Gas Mark 7 for about 12 minutes until heated through and crispy.

Makes about 36 and serves 12

2oz (50g) butter
½ pint (300 ml) water
4oz (100g) self-raising flour
2 egg yolks
2 eggs
4oz (100g) well flavoured Cheddar cheese, grated
salt
freshly ground black pepper
oil, for deep-frying

Fishy Boats

For the boats
6oz (175g) plain flour
1½oz (40g) lard
1½oz (40g) margarine
about 1 tablespoon cold water

These little pastry boats should be filled just before serving so that the pastry stays nice and crisp. I give a selection of fillings below.

Heat the oven to 400°F/200°C/Gas Mark 6.

Measure the flour into a bowl and rub in the fats until the mixture resembles fine breadcrumbs. Mix with sufficient water to give a firm dough, knead lightly until smooth then roll out on a lightly floured surface. Use to line as many small boat moulds as you have (or a patty tin will work as well). Arrange the pastry-filled boats on a baking tray, line each with a small piece of foil then bake in the oven for about 10 minutes. Remove the foil and continue to bake for a further 10 minutes or until all the pastry is cooked. Allow to cool, then lift out and repeat until all the pastry has been used.

Fill with a variety of the freshly made fish fillings just before serving.

Prawn and Mayonnaise

Mix 6oz (175g) peeled prawns with ¼ pint (150ml) mayonnaise, a tablespoon freshly chopped parsley and a little lemon juice, salt and pepper to taste.

Crab

Mix 4oz (100g) prepared crab meat with 2oz (50g) very finely chopped cucumber, a little lemon juice, salt, pepper and ¼ pint (150ml) good thick mayonnaise.

Tuna

Mix 4oz (100g) drained canned tuna with a little French dressing, salt, pepper and 3oz (75g) very finely chopped onion.

Makes about 24 boats, depending on the mould size

Cheese Filo Puffs

Filo *pastry or paste can also be seen as* fillo *or* phyllo, *but they are all the same, just spelt differently! It is available from delicatessens, continental grocers and some good supermarkets in sheets. It freezes well.*
Prepare these puffs in advance and bake as needed. Serve warm.

Heat the oven to 400°F/200°C/Gas Mark 6. Lightly grease two large baking sheets.

Start by preparing the filling. Melt the butter in a pan, stir in the flour and cook for a minute then gradually blend in the milk. Bring to the boil, stirring until smooth and thickened. Remove from the heat and season with salt, pepper, nutmeg and mustard. Stir in the cheese until it has melted.

To assemble the puffs, carefully unroll the pastry. Take one sheet and brush over it evenly with melted butter. Cut the pastry into 2½ inch (6cm) strips. Spoon a little of the sauce on to one corner of the strip of pastry, and fold this corner over to form a triangle. Keep folding the triangle over until the end of the strip is reached and the filling is secured in the centre. Repeat until each of the butter-softened pastry sheets and all the filling have been used. Arrange on the baking sheets, brush with more melted butter and bake in the oven for about 5–10 minutes until crisp and golden brown. Serve warm.

Makes about 25

1lb (450g) packet of filo pastry
6oz (175g) unsalted butter, melted

For the filling
2oz (50g) butter
2oz (50g) flour
½ pint (300 ml) milk
salt
freshly ground black pepper
freshly grated nutmeg
1 teaspoon Dijon mustard
8 oz (225g) well flavoured Cheddar cheese, grated

Hot Vol-au-Vents

Vol-au-vents are always popular to serve for a buffet. I find it takes too much time to make my own cases — all that cutting out! — so I usually buy the frozen cases then bake and fill them at home. Follow the instructions on the side of the packet. Fill them when baked with one of the two good sauces below, then heat them in the oven at 400°F/200°C/Gas Mark 6 for about 20 minutes before serving. Each of the sauces will fill about 12 medium vol-au-vent cases.

Cheese and Ham

1oz (25g) butter
1oz (25g) flour
½ pint (300ml) milk
salt
freshly ground black pepper
1 teaspoon Dijon mustard
a little grated nutmeg
3oz (75g) well flavoured
  Cheddar cheese, grated
3oz (75g) ham, finely chopped

Heat the butter in a pan, add the flour and cook for a minute, then gradually blend in the milk. Bring to the boil, stirring until thickened. Remove from the heat and stir in the seasoning, mustard, nutmeg, cheese and ham. Allow to cool then use to fill the vol-au-vents just before reheating as suggested above.

Prawn

1 oz (25g) butter
1oz (25g) flour
½ pint (300 ml) milk
salt
freshly ground black pepper
1 tablespoon tomato purée
6oz (175g) peeled prawns,
  chopped
juice of ½ lemon
1 teaspoon Worcestershire sauce

Heat the butter in a pan, stir in the flour and cook for a minute, then gradually blend in the milk. Bring to the boil, stirring until thickened. Remove from the heat and stir in the seasoning, purée, prawns, lemon juice, and Worcestershire sauce. Fill as before.

Mini Pissaladières

These tiny savoury flans are good to serve on a buffet table as they can just be picked up in the fingers for eating. It's so much easier than having to cope with slices from a large flan.

Heat the oven to 400°F/200°C/Gas Mark 6.

To make the pastry, measure the flour into a bowl and rub in the lard and margarine until the mixture resembles fine breadcrumbs. Mix to a firm dough with the water. Knead gently until smooth then roll out on a lightly floured surface and use to line twenty-four patty tins. Divide the cheese between the pastry cases and bake in the oven for about 10 minutes until the cheese has melted.

Whilst the pastry is cooking, prepare the tomato topping. Heat the butter and oil in a pan and fry the onion and celery for about 5 minutes until beginning to soften. Add the remaining ingredients and cook until the mixture has reduced to a thick pulp. Spoon the tomato mixture into the pastry cases and return to the oven for about 20 minutes until the pastry is properly cooked. Serve warm.

Makes about 24

For the pastry
8oz (225g) plain flour
2oz (50g) lard
2oz (50g) margarine
about 2½ tablespoons cold water
6oz (175g) well flavoured
    Cheddar cheese, grated

For the tomato topping
1oz (25g) butter
1 tablespoon sunflower oil
1 large onion, chopped
2 sticks of celery, chopped
14oz (396g) can of tomatoes
1 tablespoon tomato purée
1 tablespoon freshly chopped
    parsley
1 teaspoon sugar
salt
freshly ground black pepper

Cheese Almond Biscuits

These delicious crunchy cheese biscuits are good to serve with drinks.

Heat the oven to 350°F/180°C/Gas Mark 4. Lightly grease a large baking sheet.

Measure all the ingredients, except the nuts, into a large bowl and work together with a wooden spoon until blended. (Alternatively, use a processor for this.) Fill a large piping bag fitted with a ½ inch (1.25cm) plain nozzle with the biscuit mixture and pipe about 40 small blobs on the prepared baking sheet. Press a half nut in the centre of each and bake in the oven for about 20 minutes until pale golden brown. Allow to cool for a few moments on the baking sheet then lift off with a palette knife and finish cooling on a wire rack.

Makes about 40 biscuits

4oz (100g) soft margarine
2oz (50g) rice flour
3½oz (85g) self-raising flour
3oz (75g) well flavoured
    Cheddar cheese, grated
½ level teaspoon salt
½ level teaspoon dried mustard
freshly ground black pepper

For the topping
40 blanched almond halves

Home-Fried Nuts

Take a mixture of unsalted nuts such as almonds, cashews and peanuts and fry in a little butter until golden brown. Drain on kitchen paper and serve sprinkled with salt.

Quick Cocktail-Stick Snacks

Spear the following combinations of foods on to wooden cocktail sticks and serve on platters decorated with salad or parsley.

Cubes of well flavoured Cheddar cheese and ham
Cubes of blue cheese and seeded black grape halves
Small cubes of cooked chicken and dill pickles

Sardine-Stuffed Eggs

12 eggs, size 6
4 oz (120g) can sardines
1 tablespoon lemon juice
1 tablespoon mayonnaise
salt and pepper
cayenne

Buy either very small size 6 eggs or, if you can get them, use quail's eggs (they take just 2½ minutes to hard-boil).

Hard-boil 12 eggs, shell and cut in half lengthways, then scoop the yolks out into a small bowl. Add to them the contents of a drained can sardines, then mash together with 1 tablespoon lemon juice, 1 tablespoon mayonnaise and a little seasoning. Spoon the filling back into the egg-white halves and sprinkle with a little cayenne pepper.

Tiny Open Sandwiches

Use firm brown bread or Danish rye bread for this. Spread slices with a little butter and cut into mouthful-sized pieces. Top with a selection of the following toppings (or choose different ones from the Snitters on page 125).

Herring and Soured Cream

3 oz (75g) Matjes herring fillets, drained and finely chopped, mixed with 4 tablespoons soured cream, salt, pepper and ½ teaspoon ground turmeric.

Pâté

Spread with a little smoked mackerel pâté (page 125), taramasalata (page 163) or liver pâté and decorate with a few slices of radish.

Egg Mayonnaise

Roughly chop 4 hard-boiled eggs and mix with 3 tablespoons mayonnaise, 2oz (50g) cream cheese, salt and pepper. Decorate with a few snipped chives.

Brown Sugar Meringues

Use non-stick silicone paper for baking the meringues: this only needs to be brushed off after use and then it can be used time and time again. Sandwich the meringues with whipped cream just before serving as they will start to go soft if filled too soon.

4 egg whites
8oz (225g) light soft brown sugar
about ½ pint (300 ml) whipping cream, whipped

Heat the oven to 200°F/100°C/Gas Mark ¼, and line 3–4 large baking sheets with silicone paper.

Put the egg whites into a large bowl and whisk with an electric whisk on high speed until they form soft peaks. Add the sugar, a teaspoonful at a time, whisking well after each addition, until all the sugar has been added. Using 2 teaspoons, spoon the meringue out on to the baking sheets, or pipe out with a fluted nozzle into small blobs. This will give about fifty small meringues.

Bake in the oven for 3–4 hours until the meringues are firm and dry and will lift easily off the paper. Allow to cool, and just before serving sandwich the halves together with a little of the whipped cream.

Makes about 25 double meringues

Baby Chocolate Eclairs

2oz (50g) butter
¼ pint (150ml) water
2½oz (60g) plain flour
2 eggs, beaten

For the filling
½ pint (300 ml) whipping
  cream, whipped

For the icing
3oz (50g) butter
1oz (25g) cocoa, sieved
4oz (100g) icing sugar, sieved
1 tablespoon water

Always a favourite, whatever their size. These make a delicious mouthful at the end of a buffet meal.

Heat the oven to 400°F/200°C/Gas Mark 6 and lightly grease a couple of baking sheets.

Put the butter and water in a pan and bring to the boil. Remove from the heat as soon as the butter has melted and add the flour all at once. Beat until the mixture forms a ball, and comes away from the sides of the pan. Gradually beat in the eggs a little at a time until the mixture becomes a smoothy shiny paste. Turn it into a piping bag fitted with a ½ inch (1.25cm) plain icing nozzle, and pipe twenty baby eclairs, each about 1½ inches (3–4cm) long, on to the baking sheets. Bake in the oven for about 20 minutes until well risen and golden brown. Remove from the oven and split one side of each eclair so the steam can escape. Return to the oven, lowering the temperature to 350°F/180°C/Gas Mark 4, to dry out for 10 minutes. Allow to cool.

Fill each of the eclairs with a little piped or spread whipped cream. For the icing, measure the butter into a pan, heat gently until melted then stir in the cocoa and cook for a minute. Remove from the heat and stir in the icing sugar and water. Beat until smooth then dip the top of each eclair into the icing. Leave to set. Serve on the day they are filled and iced.

Makes about 20 baby eclairs

SUMMER BUFFETS

Everything you eat at a buffet must be managed with a fork, or a spoon. One is usually standing up, clutching a plate and a glass of wine, or perching on the end of a sofa or garden seat, so it's no good incorporating cold cuts from the roasting joint! Fork buffets are wonderfully easy to do because most of the dishes can be prepared ahead and then garnished just beforehand.

Most of the recipes in this section are for cold foods, which should be kept chilled until about half an hour or so before serving. But even a summer's day can be chilly. If this is likely, serve medium-sized jacket-baked potatoes or another hot potato dish with some hot vegetables. Always serve quiches hot, or at least warm, as this makes both the pastry and filling taste even better.

Puddings can be as simple or elaborate as you like. Summer is the classic time for icecreams, of which there are a selection throughout the book (look at the American Buffet introduction for hints about an ice-cream bar). Seasonal strawberries or raspberries and whipped double cream are easiest – and often the most appreciated!

White wines would be more appropriate to summer parties, but this will be a matter of taste. You'll need to have a cold box for the picnic to keep wine or beer cool. For the wedding buffet, depending on budget, a champagne to start, followed by wine for the meal, would be most traditional. Start a lunch party with a Bucks Fizz, a Kir or a Pimms with cucumber sticks and masses of mint. Or serve Sangria or a cider punch or cup throughout – refreshing and very much less expensive!

Menu

SPECIAL PICNIC PARTY FOR 12

Picnic Loaves

Mini Pissaladières
(page 25)

Green Bean, Courgette and Crispy Bacon Salad

Baby Tomatoes with Cream Cheese
(page 19)

Individual Caramel Custards

Quick Apricot Creams

Preparation Hints

Picnic Loaves

Make the day before and chill. Slice at the picnic.

Mini Pissaladières

Best made on the day, but can be prepared a couple of days in advance. The toppings can certainly be prepared beforehand. Put the little flans on a big, deep tray and cover with foil. Serve warm if possible.

Green Bean, Courgette and Crispy Bacon Salad

Best made on the day. Transport in a bowl covered with clingfilm. Make the dressing and put it in the base of the bowl with the salad piled on top. Toss at the last minute.

Baby Tomatoes with Cream Cheese

Can be made the day before and kept in the fridge.

Individual Caramel Custards

Turn out at the picnic.

Quick Apricot Creams

If set in individual dishes, these travel well.

Menu

WEDDING BUFFET LUNCH FOR 50

Fresh Scotch Salmon (use 2 × 10lb or 4.5kg salmon)

3 × Chicken and Tarragon Cream
(page 152)

2 × Rice and Shrimp Salad

12lb (5.5kg) Hot Buttered Baby New Potatoes

3 × Green Salad with Fennel

3 × Tomato and Avocado Salad

2 × Caramelised Oranges
(page 153)

2 × Red Fruit Salad with Almond Biscuits

2 × Swiss Chocolate and Orange Cake

Preparation Hints

Fresh Scotch Salmon

Cook the fish the day before; chill and glaze them on the day.

Chicken and Tarragon Cream

Make the day before and leave in the fridge.

Rice and Shrimp Salad

Make the day before and leave in the fridge.

Hot Buttered Baby New Potatoes

Potatoes are best cooked when you need them. Don't keep them hot for longer than you need as they will shrivel in their skins.

Salads

Make both the salads on the day, but the salad vegetables can be washed the day before.

Caramelised Oranges and **Red Fruit Salad**

Can be made the day before.

Almond Biscuits

Can be made well ahead.

Swiss Chocolate and Orange cake

Must be assembled on the day, but the bases can be made a week ahead and frozen, if you like.

Menu

SUMMER LUNCH PARTY FOR 24

2 × Chilled Watercress Soup

2 × Cidered Bacon with Penny's Sauce

Rice and Shrimp Salad

2 × Gruyère and Spinach Quiche

2 × Green Salad and Fennel

Garlic Bread
(page 142)

Whisky Trifle
(page 102)

Grapefruit Mousse with Lemon Thins
(page 111)

2 × Meringues

Preparation Hints

Chilled Watercress Soup

Make the day before. Serve hot if the weather is cold.

Cidered Bacon with Penny's Sauce

Can be cooked a couple of days ahead. It need not be collar of bacon, which is the best value; for a special occasion, and for larger quantities, you may like to use a 6lb (2.7kg) middle gammon.

Rice and Shrimp Salad

Make the day before and store in the fridge.

Gruyère and Spinach Quiche

Can be made the day before, but if possible serve it warm.

Green Salad with Fennel

Wash the salad ingredients the day before, but assemble it on the day.

Garlic Bread

Can be made ahead and kept in the freezer if this suits you.

Puddings

Both can be made the day before. The biscuits and meringues store well.

Chilled Watercress Soup

A really colourful refreshing soup. Serve very well chilled with crispy brown rolls and butter.

Heat the butter and oil in a large pan and gently fry the onion for about 10 minutes until soft. Roughly chop the lettuces and add to the pan with the watercress, saving a few watercress leaves for decoration. Cook for a few moments then stir in the flour. Cook for a minute or so longer then gradually blend in the stock, and bring to the boil, stirring, until thickened. Season well with salt and pepper, cover with a lid and simmer gently for about 15 minutes until the watercress is tender. Remove from the heat, cool a little and reduce to a purée in a processor or blender.

Turn into a large tureen, stir in the milk and allow to cool. Chill well in the refrigerator before serving. To serve, spoon into bowls and decorate with a swirl of cream and a scattering of the reserved watercress leaves.

2oz (50g) butter
2 tablespoons sunflower oil
2 large onions, chopped
2 lettuces
2 bunches of watercress
4oz (100g) flour
3 pints (1.75 litres) good chicken stock
salt
freshly ground black pepper
1 pint (600ml) milk

To serve
½ pint (300 ml) single cream

Fast Curried Eggs

Always a good standby to serve as a starter, these take little preparation and are a great favourite with guests. Coat the eggs with the sauce just before serving.

Cut the eggs in half lengthways and arrange on a serving dish or individual plates, cut side down. Blend the mayonnaise, mango chutney, curry powder, lemon juice, salt and pepper together in a bowl. Taste and check seasoning.

Spoon the mayonnaise over the eggs just before serving and decorate with small sprigs of watercress.

12 hard-boiled eggs
12 tablespoons good mayonnaise (page 41)
6 tablespoons mango chutney sauce, or mango chutney chopped
3 teaspoons curry powder
juice of 1 large lemon
salt
freshly ground black pepper

To decorate
watercress

Picnic Loaves

1 oz (25g) butter
1 tablespoon sunflower oil
2 medium onions, chopped
2 fat cloves of garlic, crushed
8oz (225g) button mushrooms, sliced
2lb (900g) minced beef
1lb (450g) pig's liver, very finely chopped
6oz (175g) fresh brown breadcrumbs
3 good teaspoons Dijon mustard
2 eggs, beaten
salt
freshly ground black pepper

Serve these loaves hot if eating at home, or cold to take on a picnic.

Heat the oven to 350°F/180°C/Gas Mark 4. Lightly grease two 2lb (900g) loaf tins.

Heat the butter and oil in a pan and fry the onion and garlic for about 5 minutes until beginning to soften. Add the mushrooms and cook for a further minute, then turn it all into a bowl. Add the minced beef, liver, breadcrumbs, mustard, eggs, salt and pepper. Mix well until thoroughly blended – I use my hands for this! Divide the mixture between the two prepared tins and level out evenly. Cook in the oven for about 1½ hours. To test that the loaf is cooked, pierce with a fine skewer, and if the juices run out clear then the loaf is cooked.

Serve hot with a good onion sauce and fresh green broccoli or, to serve cold, allow to cool in the tins, with small blocks or weights on top to press the loaves down. Chill in the refrigerator overnight like this before turning out and serving in slices with crisp French bread and salad.

Gruyère and Spinach Quiche

For the pastry case
8oz (225g) plain flour
2oz (50g) lard
2oz (50g) margarine
about 3 tablespoons water

For the filling
1oz (25g) butter
1 tablespoon sunflower oil
1 large onion, chopped
8oz (225g) Gruyère cheese, thinly sliced
8oz (225g) ham, chopped
4oz (100g) frozen cut-leaf spinach, thawed
4 eggs, beaten
½ pint (300 ml) milk
¼ pint (150 ml) single cream
salt and pepper

I always think that quiche is best served warm, so I cook it freshly or reheat before serving. It often finds its way into our picnic hamper if we are having a special picnic buffet and we are not going far.

Heat the oven to 425°F/220°C/Gas Mark 7 with a thick baking sheet in it.

For the pastry, put the flour in a bowl and rub in the fats until the mixture resembles fine breadcrumbs, then add the water and bind together to form a firm dough. Knead until smooth then roll out on a lightly floured surface and use to line an 11 inch (27.5cm) loose-bottomed deep flan tin. Chill in the refrigerator for about 30 minutes. Line the flan with greaseproof paper and baking beans, or with foil, and bake blind on the baking sheet in the oven for about 20 minutes. Remove the baking beans and paper or foil for the last 5 minutes so that the centre of the flan can cook through.

For the filling, heat the butter and oil in a pan and fry the onion for about 10 minutes until golden brown. Spoon it over the base of the flan. Arrange the slices of cheese on top of the onion and sprinkle the chopped ham on top of this. In a large jug mix the thoroughly drained spinach, eggs, milk, cream and seasoning until thoroughly blended then pour into the flan case.

Return the quiche to the oven, reduce the temperature to 350°F/180°C/Gas Mark 4, and cook for about 35 minutes until the filling has set. Serve in wedges either warm or cold.

Fresh Scotch Salmon

There is really nothing more special than salmon for a buffet. Scotch farmed salmon is usually a good buy all the year round, coming from the lochs of the West of Scotland where they are bred. Always remember that, like all fish, it needs very little cooking, and it should be cooked the day before.

If cooking larger salmon – for the Wedding Buffet Lunch, for instance – you will need more cucumber for decoration.

6lb (2.75kg) fresh salmon
1 onion, peeled and quartered
12 black peppercorns
2 bay leaves
4 tablespoons white wine vinegar

To decorate
½ cucumber, sliced
fresh dill or parsley

Lift the salmon into a fish kettle, and add the onion, peppercorns, bay leaves and vinegar with just enough water to cover. Put the lid on, bring slowly to the boil, then simmer gently for 12 minutes. Remove from the heat and leave until the fish is warm but not hot, which will take about 4 hours.

To cook the salmon in an oven, if you don't have a fish kettle, remove the head, season the fish well, and wrap in buttered foil. Lift into a large meat tin, and pour in sufficient boiling water to come half-way up the fish. Cook at 400°F/200°C/Gas Mark 6 for 10 minutes per pound (450g), turning the fish once during cooking. Leave the fish to become lukewarm.

Drain the fish, lift out on to a work surface, and carefully peel off the skin. Stand on a serving platter, cover with clingfilm and chill over-night or until required. To serve, decorate with slices of cucumber and fresh dill or parsley. Serve with Cucumber Mayonnaise (page 41) or with a simple sauce made by mixing ½ pint (300 ml) good mayon-naise and ½ pint (300 ml) soured cream and the juice of 1 lemon.

Pink Trout with Dill

12 pink-fleshed trout, about
    10oz (275g) each, cleaned
juice of 1 lemon
12 black peppercorns
a little salt

To serve
slices of cucumber and fresh dill

Farmed trout is now available in most parts of Britain. Although it takes time to prepare and cook the fish the day before, it means that once that is done you have no worries on the day itself. A whole fish can be served per person, or a half fish plus another dish.

Set the oven to 400°F/200°C/Gas Mark 6.

Arrange the cleaned fish in a large roasting tin, and add the lemon juice, peppercorns and salt. Cover with boiling water and a lid of foil, then poach in the oven for 30–40 minutes, until the flesh of the fish has become matt pink (test along the backbone). Remove from the oven and leave covered until lukewarm. Drain off the water. Skin each fish and discard the heads. Lift the top fillet gently off the bone, pull out the bone and then carefully replace the fillet. Carefully arrange the twelve fish on a flat tray that will go in the fridge. Cover with clingfilm and chill overnight.

The next day, arrange cucumber slices down each fish and decorate with dill. Serve with Cucumber Mayonnaise (page 41).

Badminton Chicken (or Turkey)

1 × 8–10lb (3.5–4.5kg)
    roasting chicken (or turkey)
    cooked
1 pint (600 ml) home-made or
    good bought mayonnaise
    (page 41)
3 tablespoons tomato purée
½ × 12½oz (354g) jar of
    mango chutney
juice of ½ lemon
1–2 heaped teaspoons curry
    powder
salt
freshly ground black pepper

To decorate
1 fresh mango, peeled and sliced
sprigs of parsley

So called because at short notice we decided to go to one of the three-day events. I had already cooked a large roaster chicken for the weekend but I wanted to make it more special and manageable to eat with a fork, knowing we would be standing up or balancing a plate whilst sitting on a rug. Preparing it the night before was ideal as the mild spicy flavour really penetrated the chicken. The recipe is not unlike the Cordon Bleu Coronation Chicken, but the sauce is made in 2 minutes!

Take all the skin off the bird, remove the bones and cut the meat into manageable pieces easy to eat with a fork. Use the bones for stock.

Measure the mayonnaise, purée, chutney and lemon juice into a bowl, cutting up any large pieces in the mango chutney. Add a teaspoon of curry powder to start and season well, then taste and add more curry powder if necessary. Add the chicken or turkey, cover and leave overnight in the refrigerator.

The next day, pile into a shallow serving dish, and decorate with mango slices and parsley. Good accompaniments are a rice salad and Green Salad with Fennel.

Cidered Bacon

Boned collar bacon is extremely good value for money and ideal to serve for a buffet. Prepare well in advance and then chill in the refrigerator overnight as this makes for easier carving. Serve with a Cumberland sauce or Penny's Sauce for Ham (next recipe).

3lb (1.4kg) collar of bacon joint
2 bay leaves
cider

For the glaze
2 good tablespoons demerara
  sugar
2 teaspoons dry mustard
2 good tablespoons runny honey

Stand the bacon joint in a pan, cover with cold water and leave to stand overnight. Drain the water from the joint, then add the bay leaves and sufficient cider just to cover the joint. Bring to the boil, cover with a lid and simmer very gently for 20 minutes per pound (450g) plus an extra 20 minutes – about an hour in all. Do simmer gently otherwise the meat will toughen and shrink. When the meat is tender, lift out of the pan and leave until cool enough to handle. Lift off the skin with a small sharp knife, then mark the fat into a criss-cross of diamond shapes.

   Mix together the ingredients for the glaze and pat on to the surface of the fat. Cover the lean parts of the joint with foil and cook in a very hot oven at 450°F/230°C/Gas Mark 8 for about 10 minutes until evenly browned. Allow to cool then wrap in foil and chill in the refrigerator before carving.

Penny's Sauce for Ham

This recipe was given to me by a very great girlfriend. It is an excellent accompaniment to cold ham and can be made in advance.

8oz (225g) dark muscovado
  sugar
2oz (50g) made English mustard
1/2 pint (300 ml) sunflower oil
salt
freshly ground black pepper
1/4 pint (150 ml) inexpensive red
  wine

Measure all the ingredients into a processor or blender and process for a few seconds until thoroughly blended. Taste to check seasoning then pour into a serving bowl.

Hot Buttered Baby New Potatoes

3lb (1.4kg) baby new potatoes,
   washed and scraped
salt
butter
a few sprigs of mint
finely chopped parsley

Tiny new potatoes are now available most of the year. Marks and Spencer have the best flavoured ones – and they are clean too!

Remember that larger parties tend to eat less, so when multiplying, knock off about 10 per cent. For a party for fifty, 12lb (5.5kg) of these potatoes will be quite adequate.

Cook the scraped potatoes in boiling salted water until just tender and then drain. Add butter and the mint, toss well, cover with the lid and keep hot (but not for too long, as the skins will wrinkle).

Just before serving, turn into a serving dish and sprinkle with masses of chopped parsley.

Green Bean, Courgette and Crispy Bacon Salad

1½lb (675g) green beans
12oz (350g) courgettes, sliced
6 tablespoons French dressing
   (page 42)
8oz (225g) thinly sliced streaky
   bacon
freshly chopped parsley

This is good to serve in the summer when you perhaps have beans and courgettes in the garden. The recipe can be prepared either with runner beans or the little French beans, depending on which are most readily available.

Top and tail French beans; if you use long runner beans, then slice them as well. Blanch the beans in a pan of boiling salted water for about 5 minutes, so that they are still crisp in the middle, then drain and refresh under running cold water. Transfer to a bowl and add the sliced courgettes and French dressing. Leave to stand whilst preparing the bacon.

Cut the bacon into small strips then grill or fry in a non-stick pan until crisp. Allow to cool. Add to the bean mixture and toss together. Turn into a serving dish and serve sprinkled with freshly chopped parsley.

March House Salad

It is not essential to include the water chestnuts, but I do find that they add to the texture of the salad. Use a nice large glass bowl to serve, as it's attractive to see the layers of peas and salad with mayonnaise on top.

Toss the lettuce, onions, water chestnuts and celery together in a large glass serving bowl. Blanch the peas in a pan of boiling salted water for a few moments until bright green in colour, then refresh under running cold water. Drain thoroughly, and make a thick layer of them on top of the tossed salad.

For the topping, blend all the ingredients together in a bowl then spoon evenly over the peas. Cover with clingfilm and stand in the refrigerator for about 4 hours before serving.

1 medium iceberg lettuce, shredded
6 spring onions, chopped
1 × 8oz (225g) can of water chestnuts, drained and sliced
3 sticks of celery, chopped
10oz (275g) frozen peas

For the topping
½ pint (300 ml) good thick mayonnaise (page 41)
2 teaspoons caster sugar
2oz (50g) Parmesan cheese, grated
salt
2 fat cloves of garlic, crushed
freshly ground black pepper

Green Salad with Fennel

This is quite one of my favourite salads. The fennel really does lift an ordinary green salad.

Place the fennel, celery and dressing in a bowl. Cover with clingfilm and chill in the refrigerator for about 2 hours. To assemble the salad, wash and drain the lettuces and break into small pieces into a serving bowl. Slice the cucumber, cut the pepper into thin strips after discarding the seeds and pith, and wash the watercress. Add all these to the lettuce.

Just before serving add the fennel, celery and dressing and toss together. Serve straightaway. The dressing should not be added to the salad too soon before serving otherwise the lettuce will begin to go limp.

1 head of fennel, thinly sliced
6 sticks of celery, chopped
6 tablespoons French dressing (page 42)
2 lettuces
1 cucumber
1 small green pepper
1 bunch of watercress

Tomato and Avocado Salad

3 large avocado pears
juice of ½ lemon
2lb (900g) firm tomatoes,
  skinned and sliced
good ¼ pint (150ml) French
  dressing (page 42)

A gloriously colourful salad. I find it best to buy avocados a few days in advance and then leave them on a sunny windowsill to ensure they are ripe when I need them.

Peel the avocado pears, cut in half, and remove stones. Slice and toss in lemon juice to prevent them from discolouring. Arrange the tomato slices on a large serving platter and arrange the slices of avocado on top of this. Spoon over the French dressing and serve.

Serves 12, with a choice of other salads

Rice and Shrimp Salad

1lb (450g) long-grain rice
1 large red pepper, seeded and
  chopped
6 spring onions, finely sliced
12oz (350g) peeled shrimps
2 teaspoons paprika
2 teaspoons dry mustard
salt
freshly ground black pepper
1 tablespoon caster sugar
2 good tablespoons freshly
  chopped mint
scant ¼ pint (150ml) sunflower
  oil
3 tablespoons white wine vinegar
juice of 1 orange
a few drops of Tabasco

Do not use dried mint instead of fresh as it does not work nearly as well. Use a few freshly snipped chives instead, if you have them.

Cook the rice in boiling salted water until just tender. Drain and rinse under running warm water, then drain thoroughly. Turn the rice into a large bowl and stir in the chopped pepper, spring onions and shrimps. In another bowl blend together all the remaining ingredients then pour over the rice mixture and mix well.

Cover with clingfilm and chill in the refrigerator for about 3 hours. Taste to check seasoning, then transfer to a clean serving bowl.

Serves 12, with a choice of other salads

Mayonnaise

I now make all my mayonnaise using whole eggs and a processor. It really is foolproof!

Put all the ingredients, except the oil and lemon juice, in a processor or blender and switch on to a low speed to blend. Turn up to the fastest speed and add the oil in a slow steady stream until the mixture is very thick and all the oil has been absorbed. Add the lemon juice and process until thoroughly mixed. Taste and check seasoning.

Makes 1½ pints (900ml)

2 eggs
2 tablespoons white wine vinegar
1 teaspoon caster sugar
1 teaspoon dry mustard
1 teaspoon salt
freshly ground black pepper
about 1 pint (600ml) sunflower
*   oil*
juice of 1 lemon

Curry

Sauté 1 small chopped onion and a clove of crushed garlic in a little butter until soft, then add 1 tablespoon tomato purée, ½ level teaspoon curry powder, 1 tablespoon lemon juice and 2 tablespoons apricot jam. Heat gently until jam has melted then purée in a blender until smooth. Allow to cool and stir into ½ pint (300 ml) mayonnaise.

Dill

Stir 2 tablespoons double cream and 2 tablespoons freshly chopped dill into ½ pint (300 ml) mayonnaise.

Cucumber Mayonnaise

The perfect accompaniment to cold trout and salmon dishes. Peel a cucumber and cut the flesh into small cubes. Mix into 1 pint (600 ml) mayonnaise with 2 tablespoons dill, freshly snipped, and season to taste with salt and pepper.

French Dressing

¼ pint (150 ml) sunflower oil
2 fat cloves of garlic, crushed
½ teaspoon dry mustard
salt
freshly ground black pepper
about 6 tablespoons white wine
   or cider vinegar

Good with any variety of salads, this dressing is particularly nice tossed in with a fresh green salad. It can also be made in a processor or blender.

Measure all the ingredients into a clean empty jam jar with a screw-top lid. Twist the lid on firmly and shake vigorously until thoroughly blended. Pour over green and mixed salads and toss just before serving.

   Kept in a screw-top jar like this, the dressing will keep in the refrigerator for up to a month.

Makes about ½ pint (300 ml)

Nicola's Wholewheat Bread

¾ pint (450 ml) plus 5
   tablespoons hand-hot water
1 level tablespoon black treacle
1oz (25g) fresh yeast
1½lb (675g) wholewheat flour
2 teaspoons salt
1½oz (40g) lard

We often stay on a farm in Devon where all the bread is made by Nicola. Expect a close texture as it is 100 per cent wholewheat. For a lighter texture use half strong plain flour and half wholewheat flour and a little less liquid. Serve with cheese on your buffet table.

Measure the water and treacle into a measuring jug, crumble in the yeast and mix well together. Sprinkle a little of the flour on top and leave for about 10 minutes until frothy.

   Measure the flour and salt into a large mixing bowl and rub in the lard. (This can be done in a mixer or processor.) Work all the yeast mixture into the flour and knead well. Put in a large oiled polythene bag and leave until risen to double the size: this will take about 35 minutes in a warm place, longer in a cooler room.

   Knead the risen dough again and divide in half. Shape each into a sausage shape and put in two greased 2lb (900g) loaf tins. Cover and leave to prove for about 20 minutes until double in size. Bake in the oven at 425°F/220°C/Gas Mark 7 for about 30 minutes until the loaves sound hollow when tapped underneath. Allow to cool on a wire rack out of the tins.

Makes 2 loaves

Swiss Chocolate and Orange Cake

I often make this cake to serve on a buffet table when I am offering a choice of puddings. The cake is deliciously rich so will easily serve eight (it could of course cut into more slices). It can be made well ahead and kept in the refrigerator until required.

Heat the oven to 375°F/190°C/Gas Mark 5. Grease and line with greased greaseproof paper two 8 inch (20cm) sandwich tins.

Break the eggs into a bowl, add the sugar and whisk with an electric whisk for about 5 minutes until thick and the whisk leaves a trail when lifted out. Gently fold in the flour and orange rind, then divide between the two tins. Level out evenly and bake in the oven for about 20 minutes until pale golden brown and the top of the sponge springs back when lightly pressed with a finger. Leave to cool in the tins for a few moments then turn out, peel off the paper and finish cooling on a wire rack.

For the filling and topping, place the chocolate, orange juice and oil in a bowl and stand over a pan of simmering water until melted. Remove from the heat and beat in the icing sugar until smooth. Allow to cool but not set and spread evenly over the two sponges. When set, sandwich the two sponges together with the whipped cream so there is a layer of chocolate in the middle and on top of the sponge. If liked, for a very special occasion, like the Wedding Buffet Lunch, decorate with a few fresh flowers such as primroses, japonica or dog roses just before serving.

Serves 8

3 eggs
3oz (75g) caster sugar
3oz (75g) self-raising flour
grated rind of 1 orange

For the filling and topping
6oz (175g) plain chocolate,
  broken into small pieces
juice of 1 orange
1 teaspoon sunflower oil
2oz (50g) icing sugar, sieved
½ pint (300 ml) whipping
  cream, whipped

Individual Caramel Custards

6oz (175g) granulated sugar
6 tablespoons water
butter
10 eggs, beaten
4oz (100g) caster sugar
a few drops of vanilla essence
2½ pints (1.5 litres) milk

These are best made individually as they are easiest to serve. Turn out just before serving otherwise the caramel topping fades in colour and loses its brilliant mahogany colour.

Heat the oven to 300°F/150°C/Gas Mark 2.

To make the caramel, measure the granulated sugar and water into a heavy pan and heat gently until the sugar has dissolved. Bring to the boil and boil until the syrup is a pale golden brown. Remove from the heat and divide between eighteen ramekin dishes. When cool, butter the sides of the ramekins above the caramel.

For the custard, mix the eggs, caster sugar and vanilla essence together. Warm the milk in a pan until it is hand hot then pour on to the egg mixture, stirring constantly.

Strain the custard into the ramekins and arrange in a very large roasting tin (you may have to use two tins with this number of ramekins). Fill the tin with hot water so it comes half-way up the sides of the ramekins and bake in the oven for about an hour or until a thin knife tip – inserted into the middle of the caramel custard – comes out clean. Remove from the oven and allow to cool. Chill in the refrigerator overnight, and before serving, turn each custard out on to a small plate.

Makes about 18

Quick Apricot Creams

2 packets of lemon jelly, broken into cubes
2 × 14.8oz (420g) cans of apricot halves' drained, and juice reserved
about ½ pint (300 ml) cold water
1 large can of evaporated milk
juice of 1 lemon
¼ pint (150 ml) whipping cream, whipped

Really speedy to prepare and inexpensive too. If you do not possess twelve ramekin dishes, then the creams can be served in individual glasses or small glass bowls.

Measure the jelly into a pan with the juices from the apricots made up to 1 pint (600 ml) with the water. Heat gently until the jelly has dissolved. Put the apricots into a processor or blender and reduce to a purée. Add the jelly, liquid contents of the can of evaporated milk and the lemon juice and process until smooth and evenly blended.

Pour into twelve small individual serving dishes such as ramekins and chill in the refrigerator until required. Decorate with a swirl of cream just before serving.

Wild Bramble Mousse

Prepare the mousse in individual ramekin dishes the day before, then turn out on to serving dishes an hour before serving and decorate as suggested. The mousses will stand for some time once decorated but the longer they are allowed to stand the darker a shade of pink the cream will become.

3lb (1.4kg) blackberries
12oz (350g) caster sugar
juice of 1 large lemon
6 tablespoons cold water
1oz (25g) gelatine
½ pint (300 ml) double cream
4 egg whites

To decorate
½ pint (300 ml) single cream

Put the blackberries in a pan with the sugar and lemon juice. Cover with a lid and cook over a low heat for about 15 minutes until the blackberries are soft and the juice is beginning to run out. Reduce to a purée in a processor or blender then sieve to remove the seeds. Pour ⅔ of the purée into a large bowl and reserve ⅓ of the purée to decorate.

Put the water in a small bowl and sprinkle the gelatine on top. Leave to stand on one side for about 3 minutes to form a sponge. Heat the bowl over a pan of simmering water until the gelatine has dissolved. Allow to cool slightly, then stir into the larger quantity of fruit purée. Leave on one side until cold and just beginning to thicken.

Lightly whisk the double cream until it forms soft peaks and whisk the egg whites with an electric whisk until they form peaks. Fold them both into the slightly thickened purée until blended. Divide between twelve individual ramekin dishes and leave in a cool place to set.

An hour before serving, turn out the mousses on to flat serving plates (it may be necessary to dip the bottom of the ramekins into hot water just for a second to help loosen the mousse). Pour a little of the reserved purée around each mousse. Pour the single cream into a greaseproof paper piping bag, snip the end and trail three rings of cream around each mousse on top of the surrounding purée. Drag a fine skewer carefully in lines from the mousse to the edge of the purée about 1 inch (2.5cm) apart. Then between these lines drag the skewer in the opposite direction, from the edge of the purée to the mousse, to give a 'feathering' effect. Serve as soon as possible.

Meringues

4 egg whites
8oz (225g) caster sugar
about ½ pint (300ml) whipping
  cream

These look wonderful served piled in a huge pyramid on a serving platter.
Make them in advance, but fill only a short while before serving.

Heat the oven to 200°F/100°C/Gas Mark ¼ and line two baking sheets with silicone paper.

Place the egg whites in a large bowl and whisk on high speed with an electric whisk until they form soft peaks. Add the sugar, a teaspoonful at a time, whisking well after each addition, until all the sugar has been added. Using 2 dessertspoons, spoon the meringue out onto the baking sheets, putting twelve meringues on each tray.

Bake in the oven for 3–4 hours until the meringues are firm and dry and will lift easily from the silicone paper. They will be a very pale off-white.

Whisk the cream until thick and use it to sandwich the meringues together.

Makes 12 double meringues

Red Fruit Salad

1lb (450g) rhubarb, cut into
  short lengths
1lb (450g) blackcurrants, topped
  and tailed
1lb (450g) granulated sugar
⅓ pint (200 ml) water
1lb (450g) small strawberries,
  hulled
1lb (450g) raspberries, hulled

Fruit salad always makes an excellent end to a meal. It can be prepared well ahead and chilled in the refrigerator until required. Serve with whipped cream.

Measure the rhubarb and blackcurrants into a pan with the sugar and water, and bring to the boil. Reduce the heat and simmer gently until the fruits are just tender. Stir in the strawberries and raspberries and cook for a further minute. Remove from the heat, allow to cool, then turn into a glass serving bowl. Cover with clingfilm and chill in the refrigerator until required. Serve really cold.

Chocolate Fresh Fruits

Nice to offer with a cup of coffee at the end of a meal and they are also useful for decorating trifles, pavlovas and fresh cream cakes.

fresh strawberries
*firm pears, peeled, cored and
    sliced*
under-ripe bananas, sliced
seedless grapes
cherries
plain chocolate, melted

Choose a variety of fruits from the list, remembering that the chocolate will not stick to fruits which are too wet. Prepare each fruit accordingly: the strawberries are best left with their stalks on, and only half coated with chocolate.

To coat the fruits, stab the fruit with a cocktail stick and dip into the melted chocolate. (Cherries, of course, often have their own stalk.) Allow any excess to drip back, then stand the fruits on silicone paper to set. Serve them on their cocktail sticks to save sticky fingers. Best eaten fairly soon after they are made.

Anne Goss's Almond Biscuits

Delicious served with fruit salad and any left over are good for the biscuit tin. If liked, the biscuits can be sprinkled just before baking with a little nib sugar (from your baker, or crush cube sugar) or decorated with a flaked almond.

6oz (175g) self-raising flour
3oz (75g) caster sugar
2oz (50g) ground almonds
5oz (150g) soft margarine
3 drops of almond essence

Heat the oven to 325°F/160°C/Gas Mark 3, and lightly grease two large baking sheets.

Measure the flour, sugar and ground almonds into a bowl and rub in the margarine until the mixture resemble fine breadcrumbs. Add the essence and bind together. Knead lightly until smooth then divide in half, and with lightly floured hands roll each piece into a sausage shape about 1½ inches (4cm) in diameter. Wrap each in clingfilm and chill in the refrigerator for a few minutes until firm. Cut into slices and arrange on the baking sheets, leaving a little room for them to spread. Bake in the oven for about 15 minutes until just beginning to colour then allow to cool on the trays for a few moments. Lift off with a palette knife and finish cooling on a wire rack. Keep in a tin.

Makes about 40 biscuits

Lemon Thins

8oz (225g) butter, softened
8oz (225g) caster sugar
1 egg, beaten
grated rind of 1 lemon
juice of ½ lemon
10oz (275g) self-raising flour

Lovely crisp lemon biscuits, just right to serve with fruit salads, syllabubs and icecreams. If you are not terribly happy about piping, roll the mixture into two sausage shapes about 2 inches (5cm) wide, wrap in clingfilm and chill overnight then thinly slice into rounds, arrange on the baking sheets and cook as suggested in the recipe.

Heat the oven to 375°F/190°C/Gas Mark 5, and lightly grease two to three large baking sheets.

Measure the butter and sugar into a large mixing bowl, and cream together until light. Beat in the egg, lemon rind and juice, and then work in the flour until smooth. Turn the mixture into a piping bag fitted with a ½ inch (1.25cm) plain piping nozzle, and pipe small blobs on the prepared baking sheets, leaving room in between for the biscuits to spread. Bake in the oven for 8–10 minutes until just tinged golden brown at the edges then remove from the oven. Allow to cool for a few moments then lift off with a palette knife on to a cooling tray.

Makes about 70 small biscuits

WINTER BUFFETS

Winter parties conjure up visions of warming casseroles, steaming soups and satisfying puddings. All of these are here in abundance, but I've also included a cold winter menu as not everyone likes to prepare hot food (some even find it daunting).

Hot food is often easier than having a wide range of cold dishes. How many main dishes you prepare will depend on how simple you want the meal to be. If it is perhaps just something hot to have when a crowd of you come back after a picnic lunch at a race meeting or rugby match, then I would choose only one dish such as Moussaka or Beef in Horseradish Cream. With the first I would serve a green salad and garlic bread; with the latter I would serve mashed potatoes and a green vegetable. But for a more special occasion, I would choose two hot main dishes served with the same salad or vegetables. It all gets too complicated if you have to say that one vegetable goes with one main dish – the broccoli and oven-baked potatoes with the chicken, say, and the fennel dish with the beef!

There are puddings galore throughout the book from which to choose. Hot might seem more appropriate, but cold puddings are generally very much easier as most can be prepared in advance.

Mulled wine would be a good pre-meal drink on a cold winter night, but the celebratory champagne or sparkling wine drinks are always relevant and welcoming.

Menu

CHRISTMAS PARTY FOR 24

2 × Smoked Salmon Pâté

Beef in Horseradish Cream

Chicken Diana

24 Baked Potatoes

2 × Peas and Mangetouts

Grapefruit Mousse *(page 111)* **and Anne Goss's Almond Biscuits**
(page 47)

Gâteau Queen Victoria *(page 92)*

Preparation Hints

Smoked Salmon Pâté

Most fish pâtés freeze beautifully and this one is no exception. Serve it with either brown toast (difficult to make for a crowd) or small brown rolls.

Beef in Horseradish Cream

Inexpensive to make and very warming. Make it in advance.

Chicken Diana

Very simple and very quick. Best made on the day – it is something you can toss together at the last moment.

Baked Potatoes

Serve one per person. They can be scrubbed and pricked well ahead of time. Don't overcook them or keep them hot for too long as the skins can either become hard, if overcooked, or a bit wrinkled if kept in a cool oven.

Peas and Mangetouts

Prepare the mangetouts in the afternoon, but cook just before serving.

Grapefruit Mousse

Beautifully light. Freeze for a week or two if you like, and decorate with a little cream when it comes out of the freezer. The Almond biscuits can be made and stored in a tin.

Gâteau Queen Victoria

Really a chocolate roulade mixture made in round tins. It can be made totally the day before and kept in the fridge.

Menu

COLD FORK BUFFET FOR 12

Creamed Parsnip Soup

Badminton Chicken
(page 36)

½ × Pink Trout with Dill
(page 36)

Cucumber and Dill Salad
(page 129)

Winter Vegetable Salad

American Iceberg Salad
(page 109)

Hot Buttered Baby New Potatoes
(page 38)

Old English Apple Pie

Wild Bramble Mousse
(page 45)

Preparation Hints

Creamed Parsnip Soup

Can be made ahead and frozen, if you want. It makes a warming starter to the meal.

Badminton Chicken

Very easy and quick to assemble the day before. Best left in the fridge overnight so that all the flavours and spices can mellow.

Pink Trout with Dill

Serve a half trout per person. It goes particularly well with the chicken because it has a sauce. It can be prepared the day before if need be.

Salads

All the salads are best made on the day.

Hot Buttered Baby New Potatoes

Use 3 lb (1½ kg) and cook them when you need them. They will shrivel in their skins if kept hot for too long.

Old English Apple Pie

Can be made ahead and reheated, or served cold.

Menu

KITCHEN FORK SUPPER FOR 12

Mushroom Koulibiac or Spring Lamb Hotpot

Cabbage au Gratin

Minted petits pois (2 lb or 900 g frozen peas)

Apricot and Almond Flan

Old Rectory Bananas

Preparations Hints

Cabbage au Gratin

A little like cauliflower cheese. Don't overcook the cabbage, particularly if you are going to have to reheat it. Make ahead and heat in a hot oven for 30 minutes.

Minted Petits Pois

Added sautéed diced celeriac would add a little extra something. Use 2 lb (900 g) frozen petits pois.

Apricot and Almond Flan

Make ahead and slice just before serving.

Old Rectory Bananas

Make them in the morning and decorated just before serving.

Mushroom Koulibiac

Can be made ahead of time, and is very satisfactory if frozen for a couple of weeks.

Spring Lamb Hotpot

Should be assembled on the day. Very easy, simple country food.

Menu

LATE-NIGHT SUPPER FOR 12

Cheese and Pineapple Chicken

or Moussaka
(page 164)

Green Salad with Fennel
(page 39)

French bread

Iced Lemon Flummery
(page 91)

Preparation Hints

*This is a menu which can be planned well ahead, with a day
allowed for thawing. All you have to do is bake either or both
the main dishes when you get in, while your guests are having a drink.*

**Cheese and Pineapple
Chicken** and **Moussaka**

Both freeze like a dream.
Take from the freezer the day
before.

Green Salad with Fennel

It will only take you a minute
to prepare this while the main
courses are heating.

French Bread

Crisp this up in the oven for a
few minutes if necessary.

Iced Lemon Flummery

Also freezes well, but remove
from freezer before you go
out, and leave in the fridge.

Creamed Parsnip Soup

4oz (100g) butter
2 tablespoons sunflower oil
2 large onions, chopped
2lb (900g) parsnips, peeled and
    cubed
2oz (50g) flour
2 good teaspoons curry powder
4 pints (2.25 litres) good beef
    stock
salt
freshly ground black pepper
½ pint (300 ml) single cream
a little freshly chopped parsley

Always a popular soup with friends, and you could serve it as a first course to any buffet party. It's very reasonable to prepare too if you have a glut of parsnips from the garden. The hint of curry makes it that bit more special.

Heat the butter and oil in a large pan and fry the onion for about 5 minutes until soft. Add the parsnip and continue to cook for a further 10 minutes. Stir in the flour and curry powder and cook for a minute, then gradually blend in the stock. Bring to the boil, stirring until thickened slightly, then cover with a lid and simmer gently for about 35 minutes until the parsnip is tender.

Reduce the soup to a purée in a processor or blender in batches. Return the soup to the pan, taste and check seasoning and reheat until piping hot. To serve, ladle into individual bowls, swirl a little cream into the top, and sprinkle with a little chopped parsley.

Carrot and Orange Soup

2oz (50g) butter
2 tablespoons sunflower oil
1lb (450g) onions, chopped
3lb (1.4kg) carrots, sliced
2 pints (1.2 litres) good chicken
    stock
salt
freshly ground black pepper
2 pints (1.2 litres) orange juice
a few freshly snipped chives

A really refreshing colourful soup. You can use the orange juice you buy in cartons.

Heat the butter and oil in a large pan and fry the onion for about 10 minutes until soft, then add the carrot and fry for a few more minutes until bright orange in colour. Add the stock and seasoning, bring to the boil, cover with a lid and simmer gently for about 30 minutes until the carrot is tender. Remove from the heat and reduce to a purée in a processor or blender; it may be necessary to do this in batches.

Return to the pan, stir in the orange juice and reheat until piping hot. Taste and check seasoning. Serve sprinkled with a few freshly snipped chives.

Smoked Salmon Pâté

This pâté is also very good made with smoked mackerel or smoked trout. When making with smoked salmon, ask at your local delicatessen for smoked salmon pieces – the offcuts from a side of smoked salmon – which are ideal for using in a pâté and are much more reasonable to buy.

1lb (450g) smoked salmon pieces
1¼lb (550g) butter, melted
8oz (225g) cream cheese
juice of 1 lemon
freshly ground black pepper
small sprigs of watercress or
parsley, to garnish

Measure the smoked salmon, 1lb (450g) of the butter, the cream cheese, lemon juice and pepper into a processor or blender and process until smooth. (It will be necessary to do this in batches if the capacity of your processor or blender is not very large.) Taste and check seasoning.

Turn the pâté into a 2 pint (1.2 litre) loaf-shaped tureen or dish. Level out evenly and pour the remaining melted butter on top. Leave in a cool place until set. Serve in spoonfuls or slices with toast and garnished with small sprigs of watercress or parsley.

Avocados Lalique

Red lumpfish roe can be bought in small jars in most supermarkets, and it is a useful thing to keep in your store cupboard to use when you are wanting to decorate something special.

6 ripe avocado pears
juice of ½ lemon
½ pint (300 ml) good thick
mayonnaise (page 41)
3 good teaspoons horseradish
cream
3 teaspoons tomato purée
3 teaspoons Worcestershire sauce
salt
freshly ground black pepper
12oz (350g) peeled prawns,
well drained

Cut the avocados in half and remove the stones. Brush the cut surfaces with lemon juice to prevent the flesh from discolouring. Measure all the remaining ingredients into a bowl along with the remaining lemon juice. Mix well then pile into the avocados. Decorate with a little red lumpfish roe and freshly chopped parsley.

To decorate
1 small jar of red lumpfish roe
chopped parsley

Chicken Diana

12 chicken breasts, skinned and
  boned
1oz (25g) butter
1 tablespoon sunflower oil
2 large onions, chopped
2 × 14oz (397g) cans of cut
  celery, drained
1 pint (600 ml) double cream
6 tablespoons brandy
salt
freshly ground black pepper
freshly chopped parsley

This recipe was given to me by a girlfriend I hadn't seen for twenty years until I bumped into her one day when shopping. She and her husband run a restaurant, and she said she'd been serving this recipe for years to customers. It is rich and expensive, but very special, and goes particularly well with rice or potatoes baked in their jackets.

Place each of the chicken breasts between two pieces of polythene and beat flat with a rolling pin. Heat the butter and oil in a large pan and fry the chicken breasts until tender and golden brown on each side. Lift on to a warmed serving dish and keep warm whilst preparing the filling.

Add the onion to the juices left in the pan and fry gently for about 10 minutes until soft. Add the celery and cook for a few more minutes then drain off any excess fat and add the cream. Bring to the boil then add the brandy and seasoning to taste. Pour over the chicken and serve sprinkled with freshly chopped parsley.

Cheese and Pineapple Chicken

4 tablespoons sunflower oil
2oz (50g) butter
12 chicken joints or chicken
  breasts, skinned
2 medium onions, sliced
4oz (100g) flour
about 1½ pints (900 ml) chicken
  stock
2 × 15oz (425g) cans of
  pineapple pieces, drained and
  juice reserved
1lb (450g) well flavoured
  Cheddar cheese, grated
salt
freshly ground black pepper

Cheese and pineapple are unusual in combination with chicken. This dish is always a favourite at parties and it is so simple to prepare. It can be made well ahead and then reheated just before serving.

Heat the oven to 350°F/180°C/Gas Mark 4.

Heat the oil and butter in a large pan and fry the chicken for about 10 minutes until golden brown; it may be necessary to do this in two batches if you haven't a large enough pan. Lift the joints out of the pan with a slotted spoon and arrange in a large ovenproof dish.

Add the onion to the fat left in the pan and cook for about 5 minutes until soft, then sprinkle in the flour and cook for a minute. Gradually blend in the stock and pineapple juice. Bring to the boil, stirring until thickened, then remove from the heat and stir in the pineapple pieces, three-quarters of the cheese, and seasoning to taste. Pour over the chicken, sprinkle with the remaining cheese and cook in the oven for about 40 minutes until the chicken is tender and the cheese has melted and is golden brown.

Serve hot with a tossed green salad and a baked potato.

Chicken with Stilton Sauce

Do take care once the Stilton has been added as it has a tendency to stick to the pan. Keep stirring!

Lift the chickens into a large pan that will just take them, and add some salt, the peppercorns, bay leaves and enough cold water just to cover the birds. Bring to the boil then cover with a lid and simmer gently for about 1–1½ hours or until the birds are tender. Lift out of the cooking water and leave until cool enough to handle. Strain the stock and reserve.

Strip the meat from the birds, removing all the skin and bones, and cut the meat into bite-sized pieces. To make the sauce, heat the butter in a large pan and fry the onion for about 10 minutes until soft. Add the Stilton and melt, stirring all the time. Stir in the flour and cook for a minute, then gradually blend in the chicken stock. Bring to the boil, stirring until thickened. Remove from the heat and stir in the seasoning, tagliatelle and cooked chicken. Turn into a large ovenproof serving dish and cover with clingfilm until required.

To serve, cook in the oven for about 40 minutes at 350°F/180°C/ Gas Mark 4 until heated through. Serve sprinkled with freshly chopped parsley.

2 chickens of about 3lb (1.4kg) or a 6lb (2.75kg) roasting chicken
salt
10 peppercorns
2 bay leaves

For the sauce
2oz (50g) butter
2 large onions, chopped
10oz (275g) Stilton cheese, crumbled
2½oz (65g) flour
2 pints (1.2 litres) stock (from cooking chicken)
salt
freshly ground black pepper
12oz (350g) tagliatelle, cooked

To serve
freshly chopped parsley

Beef in Horseradish Cream

This is one of my favourite buffet party dishes, and the flavour of the sauce is really different. It can all be prepared well in advance, with the horseradish cream stirred in at the last minute.

Cut the meat into neat 1 inch (2.5cm) cubes. Turn into a very large heatproof casserole pan and heat gently until the fat begins to run freely from the meat. Increase heat and fry until meat has browned on all sides. Add the onion, curry powder, ginger, sugar and flour and cook for a minute. Stir in the stock, Worcestershire sauce and seasoning, cover with a lid and simmer gently for about 2 hours until the meat is tender.

When ready to serve, stir in the horseradish cream and turn into a warm serving dish. Sprinkle with chopped parsley and serve at once.

4lb (1.8kg) stewing steak
1lb (450g) onions, chopped
1 tablespoon curry powder
2 teaspoons ground ginger
1 tablespoon dark muscovado sugar
3oz (75g) flour
1½ pints (900ml) good beef stock
4 tablespoons Worcestershire sauce
salt
freshly ground black pepper
3 heaped tablespoons horseradish cream
a little freshly chopped parsley

Beef in Beer with Apricots and Walnuts

2½oz (65g) seasoned flour
4lb (1.8kg) stewing steak, cubed
2 tablespoons oil
2 large onions, chopped
1 pint (600 ml) good beef stock
1 pint (600 ml) brown ale
salt
freshly ground black pepper
2oz (50g) dried apricots,
  chopped
4oz (100g) walnuts, chopped
4 tablespoons Worcestershire
  sauce

I have found that this recipe does improve with freezing so it is a good idea to make it well in advance of a party, and freeze it until required. It also saves a great deal of preparation just before the party!

Heat the oven to 350°F/180°C/Gas Mark 4.

Measure the seasoned flour into a large polythene bag, add the meat and shake well so that all the meat is evenly coated. Heat the oil in a large pan and quickly fry the meat until browned. Add the onion and continue to cook for a further 5 minutes until the onion is beginning to soften. Stir in any remaining flour then gradually blend in the stock and the brown ale. Bring to the boil, stirring until thickened. Stir in the seasoning, apricot pieces and walnuts, and turn into a large ovenproof casserole dish. Cover with a lid and cook in the oven for about 2½ hours or until the meat is tender.

Remove from the oven and stir in the Worcestershire sauce. Taste to check seasoning, then serve piping hot with baked potatoes and a green vegetable such as beans or broccoli.

Spring Lamb Hotpot

3lb (1.4kg) fillet of neck of lamb
6 large onions
1½lb (675g) carrots
2½lb (1.1kg) potatoes
salt
freshly ground black pepper
a little freshly chopped parsley

So easy to prepare and always a great favourite on a chilly day, this dish is really a meal in itself, but you could aways serve an accompanying fresh vegetable such as broccoli or petits pois.

Heat the oven to 325°F/160°C/Gas Mark 3.

Cut the lamb into neat 1 inch (2.5cm) cubes. Peel and slice the onions, carrots and potatoes. Arrange alternate layers of meat with layers of each vegetable in a large ovenproof dish, seasoning each layer with salt and pepper. Finish with a layer of potato, overlapping the slices so they completely cover the top of the dish. Pour in enough water to come about half-way up the dish. Cover with a lid and bake in the oven for an hour, remove the lid and continue to cook for about a further hour at 350°F/180°C/Gas Mark 4 or until the meat is tender and the potatoes have browned.

Serve sprinkled with freshly chopped parsley.

Mushroom Koulibiac

This dish is ideal to serve if you have invited vegetarian friends to your buffet party – but all your other guests will enjoy it too! Serve with the soured cream and a green salad. This recipe makes two large koulibiac and each will serve six people.

Cook the rice in a pan of boiling salted water, following packet directions, and then drain. Heat the butter and oil in a pan and sauté the onion until soft, then add the mushrooms and cook until they are just beginning to soften. Blanch the shredded cabbage in a pan of boiling salted water for a minute then drain well. Carefully combine the rice, onion, mushrooms, cabbage, eggs, seasoning and parsley together in a bowl.

Roll out each block of pastry separately to rectangles about 11 × 16 inches (27.5 × 40cm). Trim off a little pastry to use for decoration. Divide the rice mixture in two, and pile it down the centre of the two pieces of pastry, leaving a border of pastry round the edges. Brush these borders with beaten egg, fold over both long sides so they overlap, making a fat sausage shape. Tuck the ends under the rolls. Lift on to two baking sheets, and score across the top three or four times with a knife. Roll out the pastry trimmings and use to make a lattice over the top of the koulibiac. Brush all over with beaten egg. Bake in the oven at 400°F/200°C/Gas Mark 6 for about 40 minutes until golden brown.

Pour the melted butter and lemon juice down the scored cuts and serve with a bowl of soured cream.

8oz (225g) brown rice
2oz (50g) butter
1 tablespoon sunflower oil
2 onions, chopped
1lb (450g) button mushrooms, sliced
1 small white cabbage, shredded
6 hard-boiled eggs, roughly chopped
salt
freshly ground black pepper
2 tablespoons freshly chopped parsley
2 × 14oz (400g) packets of frozen puff pastry, thawed
1 egg, beaten

To serve
4oz (100g) butter, melted
juice of 1 lemon
½ pint (300 ml) soured cream

Baked Potatoes

Allow half a large potato or one medium-sized potato per head.

Preheat the oven to 400°F/200°C/Gas Mark 6.

Scrub the potatoes well, brush with a little oil, and bake in the oven for about 1½ hours – the cooking time will vary with the size of the potatoes.

Cut each in half, fork the inside, and serve with a little butter.

6 large or 12 medium-sized potatoes
oil
at least 6oz (175g) butter

Scalloped Potatoes with Leek Sauce

3lb (1.4kg) potatoes, peeled
4oz (100g) butter
2lb (900g) leeks, sliced
3oz (75g) flour
2 pints (1.2 litres) milk
salt
freshly ground black pepper
2 teaspoons Dijon mustard
½ teaspoon ground nutmeg
12oz (350g) well flavoured
   Cheddar cheese, grated

I like to serve this vegetable dish with slices of cold meat such as ham or beef, and a tomato salad. It can be prepared well in advance and then cooked just before serving.

Heat the oven to 375°F/190°C/Gas Mark 5. Lightly butter a large shallow ovenproof dish.

Cook the potatoes in a pan of boiling salted water for about 5 minutes until just beginning to soften on the outside. Drain and leave until cool enough to handle, then slice thinly and arrange in the bottom of the ovenproof dish.

For the sauce, heat the butter in a large pan and fry the leeks for about 10 minutes until beginning to soften. Stir in the flour, cook for a minute then gradually blend in the milk, and bring to the boil, stirring until thickened. Remove from the heat and stir in the seasoning, mustard and nutmeg. Taste and check seasoning. Pour over the potatoes and sprinkle with the grated cheese. Cook uncovered in the oven for about 40 minutes until the potatoes are tender and the cheese has melted and is golden brown on top.

Lyonnaise Potatoes

1lb (450g) onions, sliced
butter
4lb (1.8kg) potatoes, peeled and
   sliced
salt and freshly ground black
   pepper

These cook by themselves and need very little attention.

Preheat the oven to 375°F/190°C/Gas Mark 5.

Fry the sliced onions in about 2–3oz (50–75g) butter until soft. Arrange them and the sliced potatoes in a greased ovenproof dish in alternate layers, seasoning well and dotting with a little butter in between layers. Finish with a layer of neatly arranged potatoes on top and brush liberally with melted butter. Bake in the oven for about 2 hours.

Cheesy Garlic Potatoes

Preheat the oven to 375°F/190°C/Gas Mark 5.

Butter an ovenproof dish generously with about half the butter, and then spread the crushed garlic over the bottom and sides of the dish. Arrange the potatoes in layers in the dish, seasoning well between each layer with salt, pepper and a sprinkling of grated cheese.

Heat the milk until almost boiling then beat in the eggs. Pour over the potatoes. Dot with butter and sprinkle with the remaining grated cheese, and bake in the oven for about 1½ hours or until the potatoes are tender.

2oz (50g) butter
3 fat cloves of garlic, peeled and crushed
3lb (1.4kg) potatoes, peeled and thinly sliced
salt and freshly ground black pepper
about 8oz (225g) well flavoured Cheddar cheese, grated
1½ pints (900 ml) milk
2 eggs

Cabbage au Gratin

The first time I tested this recipe I served it with the Picnic Loaves (page 34) and it made a really appetising supper. It certainly livens up a cabbage. The dish can be prepared ahead and kept in the refrigerator until required. To serve, reheat in the oven to 350°F/180°C/Gas Mark 4 for about 40 minutes until heated through.

Cook the cabbage in a little boiling salted water for about 10 minutes, so that it is still crisp. Drain thoroughly.

For the sauce, melt the butter in a pan, stir in the flour and cook for a minute. Gradually blend in the milk and bring to the boil, stirring until thickened. Stir in the mustard, salt, pepper, nutmeg and half the cheese, and mix well. Toss the cooked cabbage in the sauce until thoroughly coated then turn into a warmed serving dish. Mix the remaining cheese and breadcrumbs together and sprinkle over the cabbage. Put under a hot grill for a few moments until the sauce is bubbling and the cheese and breadcrumbs are golden brown, or heat in a hot oven to 400°F/200°C/Gas Mark 6 for about 10 minutes.

1 large white cabbage, shredded

For the sauce
2oz (50g) butter
2oz (50g) flour
1 pint (600ml) milk
2 teaspoons Dijon mustard
salt
freshly ground black pepper
½ teaspoon ground nutmeg
6oz (175g) well flavoured Cheddar cheese, grated
2oz (50g) fresh white breadcrumbs

Baked Fennel with Lemon

8 fennel heads
salt
freshly ground black pepper
4oz (100g) butter
juice of 2 large lemons
a little freshly chopped parsley

Choose fennel heads which are white in colour. Those that are green tend to be a little bitter.

Heat the oven to 350°F/180°C/Gas Mark 4.

Cut each head of fennel into about six wedges and arrange in a large shallow ovenproof dish in layers, seasoning well between each layer. Dot with the butter and pour over the lemon juice. Cover with a lid or piece of foil and bake in the oven for about 1¼ hours until the fennel is tender.

Serve hot sprinkled with a little freshly chopped parsley.

Green Beans with Tomato and Onion Sauce

3lb (1.4kg) French beans
2 tablespoons sunflower oil
1 large onion, chopped
2 fat cloves of garlic, crushed
2 × 14oz (397g) cans of
    tomatoes
salt
freshly ground black pepper
1 teaspoon sugar

Take care not to overcook the beans. They should still have a crunch in the middle.

Heat the oven to 275°F/140°C/Gas Mark 1.

Trim the ends of the beans and cook in a pan of boiling salted water for about a minute then drain well and arrange in an ovenproof dish.

Heat the oil in a pan and fry the onion and garlic for about 5 minutes until beginning to soften. Add the contents of the cans of tomatoes and continue to cook without a lid until thick and pulpy. Stir in the salt, pepper and sugar and pour over the beans. Cover with a lid or piece of foil and cook in the oven for about an hour.

Peas and Mangetouts

1lb (450g) mangetouts
1½lb (675g) frozen peas or
    petits pois, thawed
a good knob of butter

Mangetouts are expensive to buy but are so nice to serve for a party. By serving them mixed with peas it stretches them that bit further and helps the cost.

You could also use sliced courgettes instead of mangetouts: Bring the peas to the boil then add to sliced courgettes, and boil for 3 minutes before draining.

Top and tail the mangetouts and string if necessary. Put into a large pan of boiling salted water with the peas. Bring back to the boil, cover with a lid and simmer gently for about 3 minutes until just tender. Drain thoroughly. Return to the pan and toss in butter over a gentle heat. Turn out into a warm serving dish to serve.

Garden Vegetables au Gratin

This really is a very versatile supper dish and I tend to use whatever vegetables I have available from the garden or those which seem the best buy in the shops. Another good combination is courgettes, cauliflower sprigs and red or green peppers.

2 tablespoons sunflower oil
1oz (25g) butter
2 large onions, chopped
3 fat cloves of garlic, crushed
2lb (900g) carrots, sliced
2lb (900g) courgettes, sliced
salt
freshly ground black pepper
2lb (900g) tomatoes, skinned and sliced

Heat the oil and butter in a very large pan, and fry the onion, garlic and carrots gently for about 10 minutes until just beginning to soften. Increase the heat and add the courgettes and stir-fry with the onion and carrot for about 5 minutes. Season well. Turn into a large shallow ovenproof dish and top with the slices of tomato.

For the topping, heat the butter in a pan, add the flour and cook for a minute then gradually blend in the milk and bring to the boil, stirring until thickened. Season well with some salt and pepper, and the mustard and nutmeg, then remove from the heat and stir in the beaten eggs. Pour over the vegetables and sprinkle the top with cheese. Either brown under a hot grill or put in the oven at 400°F/200°C/Gas Mark 6 for about 20 minutes until the cheese has melted and is golden brown.

For the topping
3oz (75g) butter
3oz (75g) flour
1½ pints (900 ml) milk
2 teaspoons Dijon mustard
½ teaspoon ground nutmeg
2 eggs, beaten
6oz (175g) well flavoured Cheddar cheese, grated

Winter Vegetable Salad

4 medium carrots, peeled and
    diced
1 medium turnip, peeled and
    diced
8oz (225g) French beans,
    stringed and chopped
6 tablespoons French dressing
    (page 42)
4 medium potatoes, scrubbed
½ pint (300 ml) good thick
    mayonnaise (page 41)
salt
freshly ground black pepper
2 hard-boiled eggs
2 tablespoons freshly chopped
    parsley

This salad is good to make during the winter when fresh salad vegetables tend to be more expensive and not always at their best.

Cook the carrots, turnip and beans in boiling salted water until barely tender, then drain well and toss in French dressing whilst still warm.

Cook the potatoes in their skins in boiling salted water until tender. Cool, then remove skins and dice. When they're cold, add to the other vegetables with the mayonnaise and season to taste. Mix well and turn into a serving dish. Peel and quarter the eggs and use to decorate the salad with the chopped parsley.

Red Cabbage Salad

1½ lb (675g) red cabbage
¾ pint (450 ml) soured cream
4 teaspoons horseradish cream
1 fat clove of garlic, crushed
salt
freshly ground black pepper
2 tablespoons vinegar
3 tablespoons freshly chopped
    parsley

A particularly good salad to serve with cold meats.

Shred the cabbage very finely, and place in a bowl. Mix all the remaining ingredients together thoroughly, then pour over the cabbage and toss lightly. Chill in the refrigerator before serving.

Apricot and Almond Flan

I keep a jar of vanilla sugar in my cupboard ready for making custards. Vanilla pods are not very expensive to buy and they seem to last forever stored in the sugar. Just keep topping up the jar with more caster sugar as you use the vanilla sugar, then by the next time you need vanilla sugar, the pods will have flavoured the new sugar.

For the pastry case
8oz (225g) plain flour
5oz (150g) butter, diced
2 egg yolks
2 teaspoons caster sugar
about 1 tablespoon water

For the filling
8oz (225g) almond paste

For the custard
1 pint (600 ml) milk
4 egg yolks
1 whole egg
4oz (100g) vanilla sugar
2oz (50g) flour

Apricot topping
2 × 14½oz (411g) cans of
  apricot halves
2 rounded teaspoons arrowroot
a few flaked almonds, toasted

Start by preparing the pastry. Measure the flour into a bowl, add the butter, and rub in until the mixture resembles fine breadcrumbs. Mix the egg yolks, sugar and water, add to the mixture and bind together to form a firm dough. Knead lightly then roll out the dough thinly on a lightly floured surface and use to line a deep 11 inch (27.5cm) loose-bottomed flan tin. Chill in the refrigerator for about 30 minutes.

Heat the oven to 425°F/220°C/Gas Mark 7 with a thick baking sheet in it. Line the flan with greaseproof paper and baking beans, or a piece of foil, and bake blind in the oven on the baking sheet for about 15 minutes until it is beginning to brown at the edges. Remove the baking beans and greaseproof paper or foil, reduce the oven temperature to 375°F/190°C/Gas Mark 5 and return the flan to the oven for about a further 10 minutes until the base is cooked. Allow to cool in the tin then lift out carefully and put on a serving plate.

Place the almond paste on a surface lightly dusted with icing sugar and roll out to a round large enough to fit in the bottom of the flan. Lay the piece of almond paste in the flan.

For the custard, measure the milk into a pan and bring just to the boil. Mix the egg yolks, whole egg, sugar and flour in a bowl until blended. Pour milk on to egg mixture, whisking well. Return the mixture to the pan and stir over a low heat until thickened. Remove from heat, allow to cool, stirring occasionally, then pour into the flan case.

Drain the apricots, reserving ½ pint (300 ml) of the juice. Gradually blend the juice into the arrowroot in a pan, bring to the boil, then stir continuously until thickened. Remove from the heat. Arrange the apricots over the custard, spoon over the thickened juice to give the apricots a shine. Sprinkle with a few toasted flaked almonds, and serve in slim wedges.

Old English Apple Pie

3lb (1.4kg) cooking apples,
 peeled, cored and sliced
8oz (225g) sugar
4oz (100g) butter
2 level teaspoons ground
 cinnamon

For the pastry
1lb (450g) flour
4oz (100g) hard margarine
4oz (100g) lard
about 5 tablespoons cold water
a little beaten egg, to glaze

For twelve I usually make two 8 inch (20cm) pies on pie plates. If you don't possess two pie plates, then the pie can be baked in a large Swiss roll tin and served in squares. Serve with lashings of hot custard or vanilla icecream.

Heat the oven to 425°F/220°C/Gas Mark 7.

Measure the apples into a pan with the sugar, butter and cinnamon. Cook gently for about 10 minutes until the apples are just tender, stirring occasionally to prevent them from sticking to the bottom of the pan. Remove from the heat and leave to cool.

For the pastry, measure the flour into a bowl and rub in the fats until the mixture resembles fine breadcrumbs. Mix with sufficient water to give a firm dough. Knead until smooth then turn out onto a floured surface. Roll out half the pastry and use to line two 8 inch (20cm) pie plates. Divide the filling between the plates. Roll out the remaining pastry for the lids, moisten the edges with water, and lift on top of the pies. Seal and flute the edges, use any trimmings to decorate the pies, then brush with a little beaten egg. Bake in the oven for about 40 minutes until golden brown.

Serve hot in wedges.

Old Rectory Bananas

6oz (175g) plain chocolate
4 tablespoons water
1oz (25g) butter
9oz (250g) icing sugar, sieved
12 small, slightly under-ripe
 bananas
¾ pint (450 ml) whipping
 cream, whipped
4oz (100g) plain cooking
 chocolate

These bananas should be served on the day they are made. They look wonderful all lined up on a serving dish. I haven't known anyone refuse one yet!

Measure the chocolate, water and butter into a bowl and heat gently over a pan of simmering water until the mixture has melted. Remove from the heat and beat in the icing sugar until smooth. Pour this chocolate sauce into a shallow dish and leave until cool and thick. The sauce will not coat the bananas if it has not cooled sufficiently; it should be just beginning to set.

Dip the peeled bananas, one at a time, in the chocolate sauce, coat thoroughly, then lift out with two small skewers on to a baking sheet lined with silicone paper. Chill in the refrigerator until the sauce has set. Arrange the bananas on a serving dish and pipe a generous line of cream along each banana with a large star-shaped nozzle.

Decorate the bananas with chocolate curls. To make these, melt the cooking chocolate in a bowl over a pan of simmering water. Spread out on a marble or laminated top. Spread thinly with a palette knife and leave until just set. With a French cook's knife at an angle of 45°, push the knife forward to make chocolate curls. Lift the curls on top of the bananas. Scrap the chocolate left on the work surface back into the bowl and melt again. Drizzle this melted chocolate over the top of the bananas from a small greaseproof piping bag. Chill until required.

THE GREAT BRITISH SUNDAY LUNCH BUFFET

Many pubs and restaurants now have carveries from which they serve buffet-style roast lunches and dinners. People are served a selection of roast meats and then help themselves to a variety of vegetables and accompaniments. This is also a popular way to serve a roast from home if you do not have space to sit everyone formally around a table, perhaps, but would still like to serve a roast meal. If you are catering for a large number of people, carve some of the meats beforehand as this makes serving so much quicker and it is easier to keep pace with the guests. The carved meats can be kept warm in a low oven covered with foil.

I've prepared this section in a different way, as there are so many possibilities. Make up your own menus this time! I've given roasting instructions for all kinds of meat and poultry, but have also added some individual recipes which are good for a Sunday main course. I've also included all the traditional sauces, stuffings and accompaniments for roasts.

As far as a starter is concerned, there are many soups throughout the sections which would be appropriate. Other ideas are fresh, chilled melon, beautifully prepared and perhaps decorated with fresh orange and mint. A salad might be nice like the Tomato and Avocado Salad (page 40), or a Smoked Salmon Pâté (page 55) or Fresh Salmon Mousse (page 83).

For accompaniments, there are many vegetable recipes, but vegetable purées are fashionable at the moment, and are very easy to prepare. Indeed, for a buffet they're a splendid idea as they can be prepared ahead and then simply reheated in the oven in buttered dishes covered with foil (or even in the microwave). A good purée is Brussels sprouts, and my favourite is celeriac and potato. They all look good arranged together in a dish, showing off the various colours – the green sprouts, the white celeriac and perhaps an orange carrot or swede purée as well. It may be more trouble, but it looks pretty! Serve with one other 'normal' vegetable to give a bit of crunch.

Most vegetables and accompaniments can be prepared in advance, which is always useful when you're entertaining a crowd of people. If you find that the oven is jammed full of food, don't hesitate to roast the potatoes the day before. Under-roast them so that they are a light brown colour, then put them back in the pan with a couple of tablespoons of oil to brown and crisp on the day. They will take about 15 minutes above the roast, less on a top heat. You can also do individual Yorkshire puddings in advance. Cook them to perfection until crisp, then when you want them, put them back into their bun tins and reheat for about 8 minutes. It may sound rather unappetising, but it does work! All the sauces can be made well in advance.

Puddings for Sunday lunches can be as simple or elaborate as you care to make them. Choose one from any of the other sections, and Old Rectory Bananas (page 66) or Old English Apple Pie (page 66) would be good.

For drinks, serve wine with the meal: a crisp white with poultry, and a good red, a claret perhaps, with darker meats. Why not go to town before the meal and offer a delicious Bloody Mary? Chill a good vodka in the freezer (it doesn't freeze) and serve with plenty of pure tomato juice and some Worcestershire sauce (or some ground spices to taste) and a slice of lemon. Dip the rims of the glasses into beaten egg white and then into sea salt, and serve with an individual celery stick stirrer.

BEEF

Buy beef in roughly the following weights. With fillet, allow about 5oz (150g) raw weight per person. With topside and sirloin, allow 6–8oz (175–225g) per person of meat *off* the bone; 8–10oz (225–275g) of meat per person *with* the bone.

Fast Roasting

Ideal for the prime, more expensive cuts of beef – topside, sirloin and fore-rib. Prime cuts are best roasted uncovered in the oven to give a crisp brown meat on the outside and then you can decide how rare and pinkish or well done you require the middle. Roast beef on the bone looks wonderful and spectacular but there needs to be an expert carver with a sharp knife on hand (for parties it is often easiest to have the joint boned and rolled).

Prepare the meat by seasoning well with salt and freshly ground black pepper. Stand on a rack in a roasting tin and cook as suggested below.

Weight	Oven temperature	Cooking time	
		medium	*well done*
3lb (1.4kg)	400°F/200°C/Gas Mark 6	1hr, 30 mins	2hrs
4lb (1.8kg)	400°F/200°C/Gas Mark 6	1hr, 45 mins	2 hrs, 20 mins
over 4lb (1.8kg)	400°F/200°C/Gas Mark 6	13 mins per lb (450g)	18 mins per lb (450g)

These cooking time are for average roasts. If the joint is long and thin the cooking time should ideally be reduced by 5 minutes, and if the joint is particularly thick then the cooking time should be increased by 5 minutes. For really rare beef, cut the cooking time of the medium cooked joint by 10 minutes per lb (450g). To roast a whole fillet, use the same temperature: for rare, allow 12 minutes per lb (450g) plus 12 minutes; for medium, allow 15 minutes per lb (450g) plus 15 minutes; for well done, allow 20 minutes per lb (450g) plus 20 minutes.

To test that the joint is cooked, pierce the thickest part with a skewer; if the juices that run out are tinged with pink then the middle will be pink; if the juices are clear then the joint will be well done throughout.

Slow Roasting

This method of roasting should be used for the cheaper cuts of beef – brisket, rib and silverside. They are wrapped in foil and cooked in a slower oven for a longer period of time in order to tenderise the meat. The meat is first browned in a hot oven then covered and the temperature reduced so that the joint can cook in its own steam.

Season the joint with salt and pepper. Heat a little dripping in a roasting tin in the oven at 425°F/220°C/Gas Mark 7. Add the joint and place in the oven, turning it to brown the meat on all sides, then cover with foil and cook as follows:

Weight	Oven temperature	Cooking time:
3lb (1.4kg)	325°F/160°C/Gas Mark 3	3 hrs
4lb (1.8kg)	325°F/160°C/Gas Mark 3	4 hrs
over 4lb (1.8kg)	325°F/160°C/Gas Mark 3	1 hr per lb (450g)

With slow roasting the joint will be well done throughout. It is not possible to have the middle of the joint rare with such long cooking.

LAMB

Lamb is a very popular roast, the meat being tender and well flavoured. Roasting is suitable for all cuts of lamb except scrag and middle neck. Leg is best, though, and you should allow about 6–8oz (175–225g) raw meat per head (the smaller quantities below are for when you would like to serve a selection of meats, hot or cold). To make for easier carving, joints such as the shoulder and loin are best boned and rolled. It is not necessary to use extra fat when roasting lamb.

Season the joint with salt and pepper and sprinkle with a little dried rosemary, if liked. Stand the joint on a rack in the roasting tin and roast uncovered in the oven.

Weight	Oven temperature	Cooking time
3lb (1.4kg)	350°F/180°C/Gas Mark 4	1 hr, 40 mins
4lb (1.8kg)	350°F/180°C/Gas Mark 4	2 hrs, 10 mins
over 4lb (1.8kg)	350°F/180°C/Gas Mark 4	25 mins per lb (450g)

Cooking times do vary according to the shape of the joint. If it is particularly thick, then it may take a little longer; if a thin joint, then the cooking time may be less.

The lamb is cooked if clear juices run from the joint when pierced with a fine skewer. Some people like lamb a little pink in the centre, in which case the juices which run from the joint should be tinged with pink.

PORK

When buying a joint of pork for roasting do ask your butcher to score the rind for you. Suitable cuts of pork for roasting include loin (boned is best), leg, spare rib, and hand and spring. Allow 6–8oz (175–225g) raw weight per person.

Lift the skin off the joint with a sharp knife, then just lay on top of the joint for roasting. Brush the rind with a little oil and sprinkle with salt. Stand the joint on a rack in the roasting tin and cook as suggested below. It is not necessary to baste pork during cooking.

Weight	Oven temperature	Cooking time
3lb (1.4kg)	350°F/180°C/Gas Mark 4	2 hrs
4lb (1.8kg)	350°F/180°C/Gas Mark 4	2 hrs, 40 mins
over 4lb (1.8kg)	350°F/180°C/Gas Mark 4	30 mins per lb (450g)

Pork should never be served undercooked; to be sure, pierce with a fine skewer and if the juices clear then the joint is cooked; if they are even slightly tinged with pink, return to the oven for a little longer.

CHICKEN

Buy roasting chickens, fresh or frozen, but frozen chickens must be completely thawed before they are roasted. Allow 8–10oz (225–275g) raw weight per person. The bird should be weighed after stuffing in order to work out the cooking time. Truss with small skewers or string. Dot with a little butter and season with salt and pepper. Open roast in the oven as suggested below, basting from time to time.

Weight	Oven temperature	Cooking time
4lb (1.8kg)	400°F/200°C/Gas Mark 6	1 hr, 35 mins
5lb (2.25kg)	400°F/200°C/Gas Mark 6	2 hrs
6lb (2.7kg)	400°F/200°C/Gas Mark 6	2 hrs, 15 mins
over 6lb (2.7kg)	375°F/190°C/Gas Mark 5	20 mins per lb (450g)

To test that the chicken is cooked, pierce the thickest part of the thigh with a fine skewer and if the juices run clear then the chicken is cooked. Chicken is best left wrapped in foil to rest for 10 minutes before carving, which gives the juices a chance to settle.

TURKEY

Prepare turkey as you would a chicken but cover loosely with foil to cook. Open the foil for the last 1¼ hours cooking time to brown the skin of a large bird and for about the last 50 minutes for a small bird.

Weight	Oven temperature	Cooking time
5lb (2.25kg)	350°F/180°C/Gas Mark 4	2 hrs, 30 mins
10lb (4.5kg)	350°F/180°C/Gas Mark 4	3 hrs, 15 mins
15lb (6.75kg)	350°F/180°C/Gas Mark 4	4 hrs
20lb (9kg)	350°F/180°C/Gas Mark 4	5 hrs

A 6–8lb (2.7–3.6kg) oven-ready turkey will give 8–12 servings.
A 10–13lb (4.5–5.9kg) oven-ready turkey will give 15–20 servings.
A 14–20lb (6.3–9kg) oven-ready turkey will give 20–30 servings.

Roast Rib of Beef

When buying a fore-rib of beef do ask your butcher to saw off the vertebrae leaving them just attached and to completely remove the gristle which runs in a line underneath.

1 fore-rib of beef, about 12–14lb (5.4–6.3kg)
salt

Heat the oven to 400°F/200°C/Gas Mark 6.

Rub a little salt all over the fat on the joint. Lay the ribs in a large roasting tin with the fat side upwards and roast in the oven for 12 minutes to the lb (450g) if you like pink beef in the centre or, for a more well-done joint, roast for 14 minutes to the lb (450g). Remove the meat from the oven and allow to rest before carving. (If you want to serve cold, cool, then wrap in foil and chill in the refrigerator overnight before carving.)

To carve the joint, take the meat off the bone and then carve into slices. This is far easier than trying to carve the joint whilst it is still on the bone. Serve with Horseradish Sauce (page 78).

Serves 12 (or 16 or more if served cold with a choice of meats)

Country Pork

Get the butcher to bone the leg of pork and to score the crackling. Remove the skin from the kidneys and snip out the core with sharp scissors. Heat the oven to 350°F/180°C/Gas Mark 4.

Heat the butter and oil in a pan and fry the onion for about 5 minutes until beginning to soften. Add the mushrooms, cook for a further minute then turn into a mixing bowl, and add the breadcrumbs, parsley, sage and seasoning. Bind together with the beaten egg.

Lightly season inside the leg of pork, and spread with half the stuffing. Arrange the kidneys in a line down the middle of the stuffing then carefully pack the remaining stuffing around the kidneys.

Secure the joint with about three fine skewers. Lift into a roasting tin, rub with oil and sprinkle with a little salt. Roast in the preheated oven for about 2½ hours until the crackling is crisp, and when the meat juices run out clear after prodding with a fine skewer. Serve the pork with a thin gravy made from the juices from the meat, new potatoes and fresh green broccoli.

4lb (1.8kg) leg of pork, boned
2 pork kidneys
1oz (25g) butter
1 tablespoon sunflower oil
1 medium onion, chopped
3oz (75g) button mushrooms, sliced
4oz (100g) fresh brown breadcrumbs
1 good tablespoon freshly chopped parsley
1 teaspoon rubbed dried sage
salt
freshly ground black pepper
1 egg, beaten
a little oil

Mediterranean Lamb

1 large shoulder of lamb, boned

Stuffing
3oz (75g) dried apricots, soaked
   overnight
1oz (25g) butter
1 tablespoon sunflower oil
1 large onion, chopped
1 oz (25g) almonds, chopped
6oz (175g) brown rice
salt
freshly ground black pepper
1 tablespoon freshly chopped
   parsley

Ask your butcher to bone the joint for you, as this saves a great deal of valuable preparation time. Brown rice gives the stuffing a delicious nutty flavour. It does take much longer to cook than ordinary long-grain rice, so remember this when calculating cooking times (follow packet instructions).

Heat the oven to 375°F/190°C/Gas Mark 5.

For the stuffing, turn the apricots with their soaking water into a pan and bring to the boil. Allow to simmer for about 3 minutes until tender, then remove from the heat, strain off the water and chop. Turn them into a bowl. Heat the butter and oil in a pan and fry the onion for about 5 minutes until soft, then add to the apricots with the almonds. Cook the rice in a pan of boiling salted water until tender, strain and add to the bowl with the seasoning and parsley. Mix well.

Open out the shoulder of lamb and spoon the stuffing into the cavity, then reshape it and secure the stuffing inside with fine skewers if necessary. Weigh the joint and calculate the cooking time, allowing about 30 minutes per lb (450g) plus an extra 30 minutes. Lift into a roasting tin and roast in the preheated oven until tender: the juices should run clear when the joint is pierced with a skewer. Lift out on to a serving dish and serve with gravy and freshly cooked vegetables.

French Roast Poussin

6 poussins, each weighing about
   1lb (450g)
6oz (175g) butter
3 good tablespoons chopped
   mixed fresh herbs
3 cloves of garlic, crushed
freshly ground black pepper
1 pint (600ml) water
1oz (25g) cornflour
¼ pint (150ml) white wine

A very special dish to serve for a buffet party. This method of roasting can also be used for larger chickens, but I like to serve poussin for a real treat.

Heat the oven to 350°F/180°C/Gas Mark 4.

Wipe the poussin and remove the giblets. Cream the butter, herbs, garlic and pepper until soft and thoroughly blended. Put your hand under the skin on the breast of the poussins and work it in so that the skin is separated from the flesh. Divide the butter between each of the poussins and spread over the breast and under the skin of each bird working down over the leg joint. It is easiest to use your hand and fingers for this.

Arrange the poussins in a roasting tin with the giblets and water, cover and roast in the oven for 20 minutes then remove the cover and continue cooking for a further 25–30 minutes until golden brown and tender.

Measure the cornflour into a pan and blend with the wine. Lift the poussins out of the tin and divide each in half using a sharp pair of kitchen scissors, snipping through the breast and backbone. Arrange on a warm serving dish and keep warm. Strain the juices from the roasting tin into the pan with the cornflour and wine, and bring to the boil, stirring until thickened. Taste and adjust seasoning. Simmer for 3 minutes then pour into a sauce boat and serve with the poussins.

Roast Turkey

Serve with Chestnut Stuffing (page 76) which is cooked in the body cavity of the bird, and Sausage, Lemon and Thyme Stuffing (page 77) which is best cooked in the front end of the turkey. See page 72 for ideas on weight to buy for your numbers, and for roasting details.

Stuff the turkey, but ideally don't do this until the day you are going to roast it. The stuffings can be made a day ahead, wrapped and then stored in the refrigerator until ready to use. Brush the turkey with butter, season well and wrap loosely in foil.

Put the turkey in the oven on a shelf below the centre and roast (page 72). Open the foil for the last 1¼ hours of the cooking time for a large bird, for the last 50 minutes or so for a smaller bird. Baste from time to time.

To tell when the turkey is done, pierce the thickest part of the thigh with a fine skewer; if the juices which run out are clear, then the turkey is done. If tinged with pink return to the oven for a little longer until they are clear. After cooking, cover with foil, keep warm and allow to stand for 10 minutes before carving.

Roast Potatoes

Heat the oven to 425°F/220°C/Gas Mark 7.

Parboil the potatoes in a pan of salted boiling water for 3 minutes, then drain well. Pour the oil into a suitable sized roasting tin to a depth of ¼ inch (6mm). Heat in the oven until beginning to sizzle then add the potatoes and roast for about 1½ hours, turning occasionally, until the potatoes are crisp and golden brown.

4lb (1.8kg) old potatoes, peeled and cut into even-sized pieces
oil

Yorkshire Pudding

8oz (225g) plain flour
salt
2 eggs beaten
1 pint (600 ml) milk and water
    mixed
a little lard or dripping

The art of making a Yorkshire pudding is ensuring that the oven is hot, the batter is smooth and that the tin and fat have been thoroughly heated before adding the batter. Years ago, Yorkshire pudding was served as a first course with lashings of gravy to fill the family up before serving the meat, often in short supply. Nowadays, however, it is customary to serve the pudding with the meat and vegetables.

Heat the oven to 450°F/230°C/Gas Mark 8.
    Measure the flour and salt into a bowl. Make a well in the centre and blend in the eggs with a little of the milk and water, using a small whisk to give a smooth paste. Blend in the remaining milk and water and whisk well for a minute.
    Place a little fat in the bottom of a large shallow roasting tin, and heat in the oven until the fat has melted and is very hot. Remove from the oven and pour in the batter. Return to the oven and cook for about 25 minutes or until well risen, crisp and golden brown. Serve at once.

Chestnut Stuffing

8oz (225g) dried chestnuts,
    soaked overnight
8oz (225g) streaky bacon,
    chopped
1 large onion, chopped
1 tablespoon sugar
1oz (25g) butter
1oz (25g) porridge oats
3oz (75g) fresh white
    breadcrumbs
1 egg beaten
salt
freshly ground black pepper

Enough for a 16lb (7.2kg) turkey.

Rinse the chestnuts after soaking, and cook in boiling water for about 30 minutes until tender but still slightly crisp. Drain, cool a little and peel off any remaining bits of skin. Chop coarsely.
    Put the bacon in a non-stick pan, heat gently until the fat begins to run out, then increase the heat, and add onion and sugar. Allow to brown a little. Stir in the butter, oats, breadcrumbs and chestnuts. Remove from the heat and bind together with the egg. Season to taste and use to stuff the body cavity of the bird.

Sausage, Lemon and Thyme Stuffing

If possible do use fresh thyme and fresh parsley, they really do make all the difference. This is enough for a 16lb (7.2kg) bird.

Melt the butter in a pan and fry the onion gently until soft, for about 10 minutes. Allow to cool, stir in remaining ingredients and mix well together. Use to stuff the front end of the turkey. You can serve this stuffing separately with a roast if you like. Form into small balls with lightly floured hands and arrange in a small greased roasting tin. Cook along with the joint for about 40 minutes.

1oz (25g) butter
1 onion, chopped
1lb (450g) pork sausagemeat
4oz (100g) fresh white breadcrumbs
grated rind and juice of 1 lemon
salt
freshly ground black pepper
2 tablespoons freshly chopped parsley
1 level teaspoon freshly chopped thyme

Sage and Onion Stuffing

Measure the onions and water into a pan, bring to the boil, cover with a lid and simmer gently for about 15 minutes until the onion is tender. Drain well then stir in the sage, breadcrumbs and seasoning and mix well.

Turn the stuffing into a really well buttered ovenproof dish and level out evenly (but don't squash it down). Dot with butter and cook with the roast for about 25 minutes or until the top of the stuffing is crisp and golden brown.

2lb (900g) onions, roughly chopped
1 pint (600 ml) water
2 level teaspoons dry sage
1lb (450g) fresh white breadcrumbs
salt
freshly ground black pepper
2oz (50g) butter

Thin Gravy

Pour all the fat from the roasting tin leaving only the sediment in the bottom. Add 1½ pints (900 ml) good stock and stir well. Bring to the boil and boil for about 2 minutes until the gravy has reduced slightly. Add a little gravy browning if liked. Season and serve hot with the roast meat.

sediment from pan
1½ pints (900 ml) good stock
gravy browning (optional)
seasoning

Thick Gravy

a little fat from pan
3 level tablespoons flour
1½ pints (900 ml) good stock
gravy browning (optional)
seasoning

Pour most of the fat from the roasting tin, leaving just a little in the bottom. Stir in 3 level tablespoons flour, mix well, and cook for a minute. Gradually blend in 1½ pints (900 ml) good stock and bring to the boil stirring until thickened. Add a little gravy browning if liked. Simmer for a few moments then season to taste and serve hot with the roast meat.

Onion Gravy

Fry 1 small chopped onion in a little fat until golden brown, then add flour and continue recipe as for thick gravy.

Redcurrant Gravy

This is particularly good to serve with poultry and game. Stir a tablespoon of redcurrant jelly into the gravy and allow to melt before serving.

Horseradish Sauce

½ pint (300 ml) double cream
4 level tablespoons grated
    horseradish
2 teaspoons white wine vinegar
salt
freshly ground black pepper
a little caster sugar

My family adore horseradish and if I have any left after serving it with beef I often add a teaspoon to mayonnaise to serve with prawns or an avocado as a starter.

Measure the cream into a bowl and whisk until it forms soft peaks. Stir in the horseradish, vinegar and plenty of salt and pepper. Mix well and add a little sugar to taste. Turn the sauce into a serving dish, cover with clingfilm, and chill well in the refrigerator before serving.

Cranberry Sauce

Heat the jelly in a pan until just melted then pour into a processor or blender. Add the cranberries and the orange rind and juice and process until thick and chunky. Turn into a serving bowl and serve. The sauce can be kept for 2–3 days in the refrigerator covered with clingfilm.

1lb (450g) jar of redcurrant jelly
1lb (450g) cranberries, fresh or frozen and thawed
grated rind and juice of 1 orange

Mint Sauce

An absolute must to serve with roast lamb when the mint is first appearing in the garden in spring.

Wash and dry the mint. Strip the leaves from the stems and chop finely. Measure the sugar and boiling water into a sauce boat and stir until the sugar has dissolved. Stir in the mint and vinegar. Add a little extra sugar if necessary.

1 bunch of fresh mint (about 20 sprigs or so)
2 level tablespoons caster sugar
4 tablespoons boiling water
8 tablespoons vinegar

Bread Sauce

Stick the cloves into the onion and place in a saucepan with the milk. Bring to the boil slowly then turn off the heat and leave to stand for about 30 minutes. Lift the onion out of the milk and stir in the bread-crumbs, plenty of seasoning and the butter. Reheat until almost boiling, remove from the heat and turn into a warm serving bowl. Cover with damp greaseproof paper and keep warm until required.

4 cloves
1 large onion, peeled
1 pint (600 ml) milk
6 oz (175g) fresh white breadcrumbs
salt
freshly ground black pepper
a good knob of butter

Apple Sauce

Put the apples in a pan with the water and lemon juice. Cover with a lid and cook gently until the apples are soft and tender. Beat well until smooth then stir in the butter and sugar to taste. Turn into a serving bowl and keep warm until required.

2lb (900g) cooking apples, peeled, cored and sliced
6 tablespoons water
juice of 1 lemon
2oz (50g) butter
sugar to taste

VICTORIAN BUFFET

A party with a Victorian theme and Victorian food is good fun, and I actually gave a Victorian buffet party last year to celebrate my birthday. It was a great success and some of my guests even came dressed in Victorian costume.

I thought it a good idea to serve the quenelles and their sauce hot with brioche as the first course, as this meant that I could relax fairly quickly. The rest of the meal was cold, with the added advantage that I was able to have it all arranged on the table well before the guests started to arrive.

All the meats should be cooked at least the day before so that they can be chilled in the refrigerator overnight. This makes for easier carving. It's probably a good idea to have the meats partly carved before the party so that guests don't have to wait too long for their portion, and it's easier to keep up with demand. I chose to serve the meats with a choice of a green salad and a tomato salad, and for the puddings, I offered a wickedly fattening selection!

If this particular buffet does go to town a little, you can always serve more homely fare for a family party.

For both parties, serve Madeira or sherry before the meal, well chilled white wine and/or claret with the food, and port at the end of the meal.

Menu

VICTORIAN FAMILY SUPPER FOR 12

Leek and Stilton Soup

Wonderful Fish Pie or Steak and Kidney Pie

Puréed beetroot

Puréed carrot and swede

Buttered cabbage

Caramel Syllabub

Strawberries and cream

Preparation Hints

Leek and Stilton Soup
This can be prepared in the morning and reheated gently.

Wonderful Fish Pie
Prepare the day before and leave in the refrigerator until ready to serve.

Steak and Kidney Pie
The meat part could be prepared well ahead and frozen, but it's best to make and bake the pastry on the day.

Vegetables
The purées could have been made in the morning. Heat them through *very* gently, possibly in a double saucepan. The cabbage can have been pre-cut, but cook at the last minute.

Caramel Syllabub
Assemble just shortly before the party, but the breadcrumbs and syllabub could have been prepared earlier.

Menu

VICTORIAN BIRTHDAY PARTY FOR 24

2 × Quenelles with Spinach and Sorrel Sauce

2 × Brioches

Ballotine of Duck or Galantine of Turkey

English Ham and Cumberland Sauce
or
Roast Rib of Beef and Horseradish Sauce
(pages 89 and 73)

Selection of Salads

Hot Buttered Baby New Potatoes
(page 38)

Iced Lemon Flummery

Wild Bramble Mousse
(page 45)

Gâteau Queen Victoria

Preparation Hints

Quenelles with Spinach and Sorrel Sauce

These can be prepared a little in advance and kept in the fridge. The sauce purée can be made the day before, but the sauce itself is best made at the last minute.

Brioches

They're best freshly made, but you can reheat them.

The Main Courses

All, because they're served cold, can be prepared the day before, as can the sauces.

Salads and Vegetables

Prepare these on the day itself. Assemble, dress or cook, whichever is appropriate, just before serving.

Puddings

The Flummery and Mousse can be frozen: remember only to allow them time to come round. Make the cake the day before and store in the fridge.

Leek and Stilton Soup

This is one of the most delicious recipes for soup that I know. Do take care when cooking it as the cheese is likely to stick to the bottom of the pan. With a watchful eye and plenty of stirring, though, you can avoid this.

Heat the butter and oil in a pan and fry the leeks for about 5 minutes until soft. Add the crumbled Stilton and stir until the cheese has melted to a smooth cream. Add the flour and continue to cook for about 3 minutes, stirring all the time. Gradually add the stock and bring to the boil, stirring until thickened. Add the bay leaf and seasoning and simmer for about 20 minutes. Remove the bay leaf, taste and check seasoning. Add the cream, reheat until very hot but not quite boiling, and serve.

2oz (50g) butter
2 tablespoons sunflower oil
1lb (450g) leeks, thinly sliced
12oz (350g) Stilton cheese, crumbled
4oz (100g) flour
4 pints (2.25 litres) good chicken stock
1 bay leaf
salt
freshly ground black pepper
½ pint (300 ml) single cream

Fresh Salmon Mousse

A buffet party is an ideal occasion for serving salmon. This recipe works beautifully with the less expensive imported salmon.

Put the gelatine in a small bowl with the water, and leave to stand for about 3 minutes to form a sponge. Stand the bowl in a pan of simmering water until the gelatine has dissolved and is clear.

Pour the undiluted consommé into a bowl and stir in the gelatine. Blend the cream, mayonnaise and lemon juice together with the salmon, three-quarters of the consommé and the salt and pepper. Taste and check seasoning then pour into a 3 pint (1.75 litre) oiled ring mould. Put in the refrigerator to set. Warm through the remaining consommé so it is liquid and stir in the parsley, pour over the set mousse and return to the fridge until required.

To serve, turn out on to a serving plate and decorate with a few whole prawns. Serve with granary rolls and butter.

½oz (15g) gelatine
3 tablespoons cold water
10½oz (298g) can of condensed consommé
½ pint (300 ml) double cream, lightly whipped
¾ pint (450 ml) mayonnaise (page 41)
juice of 1 lemon
1lb (450g) cooked flaked salmon
salt
freshly ground black pepper
2 tablespoons freshly chopped parsley
a few whole prawns, to decorate

Quenelles

2lb (900g) cod fillets, skinned
   and boned
1½lb (675g) smoked mackerel
   fillets, skinned
6 egg whites
salt
freshly ground black pepper
½ teaspoon ground mace
¾ pint (450 ml) double cream

This recipe is most easily prepared in a processor but can also be prepared in batches in a blender. To prepare the quenelles ahead, poach as suggested in the recipe, arrange in an ovenproof dish, cover with foil and keep in the refrigerator until required. Reheat in the oven at 300°F/150°C/Gas Mark 2 for about 40 minutes until heated through.

Roughly chop the fish and place in a processor with the egg whites, salt, pepper and mace. Process for a few moments until absolutely smooth, then, with the processor running, add the cream in a steady stream until thoroughly blended. Take care not to over-process otherwise the cream may turn to butter. Turn the mixture into a bowl, cover with clingfilm and chill in the refrigerator for several hours before cooking.

To cook the quenelles, bring a large pan of salted water to the simmer. Dip a dessertspoon in the hot water and then take a generous spoonful of the mixture, smooth the top with another spoon and lower into the water: tap the spoon gently on the bottom of the pan and the quenelle will come away from the spoon. Poach the quenelle for 10 minutes then carefully lift out of the water with a slotted spoon, arrange in an ovenproof dish and keep warm whilst cooking the remaining mixture. Serve coated with the sauce following, sprinkled with a little freshly chopped parsley.

Spinach and Sorrel Sauce

½ pint (300 ml) white wine
2oz (50g) fresh spinach
6 leaves fresh sorrel
1½ pints (900 ml) double cream
salt
freshly ground black pepper
juice of 1 lemon

The spinach and sorrel purée can be made ahead, covered with clingfilm and kept in the refrigerator. The sauce itself should be prepared just before serving.

Pour the wine into a pan and boil rapidly until reduced to a thin syrup. Remove from the heat.

Blanch the spinach and sorrel in a pan of boiling salted water for a minute, then refresh under running cold water. Drain well. Place the spinach, sorrel and wine syrup in a processor or blender and reduce to a smooth purée.

Pour the cream into the pan in which the wine was reduced, bring to the boil, and continue to cook until the sauce will coat the back of a metal spoon. Stir in the purée and add seasoning and lemon juice to taste. Serve with the quenelles.

Brioches

Serve these in place of bread rolls with the Quenelles and Spinach and Sorrel Sauce. They are best served warm and if there happen to be any left, then they make an excellent breakfast with butter and marmalade. Use the sort of yeast you can add directly to the flour, it works a treat.

9oz (250g) strong plain white
  flour
1oz (25g) caster sugar
2oz (50g) butter
½oz (15g) easy-blend dry yeast
3 tablespoons hand-hot milk
2 eggs, beaten
a little beaten egg, to glaze

Measure the flour and sugar into a large mixing bowl and rub in the butter until the mixture resembles fine breadcrumbs. Stir in the yeast until thoroughly blended, then add the milk and eggs and work together to form a soft dough. Knead until smooth in the bowl then turn out on to a lightly floured surface and knead for at least 5 minutes. This kneading can be done in a processor and will take 60 seconds with the plastic dough blade. Return to the bowl, cover with clingfilm and leave in a warm place for about an hour until the dough has doubled in size. Lightly grease twelve fluted brioche moulds or deep fluted patty tins.

Knead the dough again on a lightly floured surface then divide into twelve equal pieces. Cut off a quarter from each piece, then form the larger part into a ball and place in the greased tins. Firmly press a hole into the centre of the ball and place the remaining small piece of dough on top of this. Cover all the brioches, once prepared, with clingfilm and leave to prove for another 45 minutes until light and puffy. Heat the oven to 450°F/230°C/Gas Mark 8.

To bake the brioches, glaze with a little beaten egg and bake in the oven for 10–12 minutes until golden brown. Gently lift out of the moulds and allow to cool on a wire rack. Serve warm with butter balls.

Makes 12

Butterballs

Use unsalted butter for this as it is the easiest to work with. Take a small knob of butter and with small butter pats work into a ball. If the butter tends to stick to the pats dampen them with cold water. Once made store the balls in a bowl of icy water until required. If you do not possess any butter pats then serve butter curls instead, by running the special corrugated implement over the top of a butter block, so the butter curls up into a roll.

Wonderful Fish Pie

3lb (1.4kg) cod fillets
freshly ground black pepper
2¼ pints (1.25 litres) milk
3oz (75g) butter
3oz (75g) flour
6oz (175g) frozen peeled
    prawns, thawed
6 tablespoons mayonnaise
    (page 41)
1 tablespoon anchovy essence
4 good tablespoons freshly
    chopped parsley
3lb (1.4kg) potatoes, cooked and
    mashed with butter and milk

Good to serve for a party as the pie can be prepared well ahead and kept in the refrigerator until required, then heated through to serve. Serve with Peas and Mangetouts (page 62) or fresh green broccoli spears.

Put the fish in a large pan, and season well with pepper. Add enough milk just to cover, then poach the fish for about 15 minutes or until the flesh flakes easily. Remove from heat and strain off the cooking liquid and reserve. Flake the fish, discarding any skin and bones.

Melt the butter in a pan, add the flour and cook for a minute. Gradually blend in the cooking liquid and the rest of the milk, then bring to the boil, stirring until thickened. Remove from the heat and stir in the fish, prawns, mayonnaise, anchovy essence, parsley and seasoning to taste. Pour this into a buttered 6 pint (3.5 litre) shallow ovenproof dish and allow to cool. Carefully spoon or pipe the mashed potato over the top of the pie.

To serve, reheat in the oven at 375°F/190°C/Gas Mark 5 for about 50 minutes, or until heated through and the potato is pale golden brown and crispy.

Galantine of Turkey

1 turkey, about 10lb (4.5kg)
1 unrolled salted ox tongue,
    about 2½lb (1.1kg), cooked
    and skinned
2 × 2½ inch (6cm) thick slices of
    ham, cut into long pencil strips

For the stuffing
2 tablespoons sunflower oil
1 medium onion, chopped
1½lb (675g) raw pork, coarsely
    minced
2oz (50g) fresh brown
    breadcrumbs
salt and black pepper
1 tablespoon chopped fresh thyme
1 egg, beaten

Be sure to chill the turkey overnight before carving as then it will hold together. When serving this for a buffet, I usually carve about half the bird before the party so that there are some slices ready to serve and then leave the remainder whole so that people can see how the turkey has been cooked; it looks so good with the tongue showing through the middle. Garnish with plenty of fresh parsley, watercress and tomatoes.

Start by boning the turkey. To do this lay the turkey breast side down on the work surface. Take a small sharp knife and make a small cut just beneath the parson's nose to release the skin then using your thumbs push the skin away from the carcass all the way down to the leg joints. Press the leg joints back against their sockets to release them, then with the knife carefully cut through the joints so that the legs are no longer attached to the carcass. Again using your thumbs, continue to push the flesh and skin away from the carcass past the oysters and then break off the backbone and remove from the bird.

Now turn the turkey over and have the breast bone facing towards you. With the knife mark down either side of the breast bone between the bone and skin and carefully push down the sides of the bone with your thumbs so that the flesh and skin come away from the bone. Continue this until the breast bone is clean then cut through the rib cage and release the breast bone.

Next remove the bones from the tops of the wings. With the knife, cut through the joint and scrape the flesh away from the rib cage and neck until all the bone has been exposed. The rib cage and neck can then easily be pulled out from the bird. Take great care all through the boning of the bird not to pierce the skin as this will spoil the cooked appearance of the bird.

For the stuffing, heat the oil in a small pan and fry the onion for about 5 minutes until beginning to soften. Measure all the other ingredients for the stuffing into a large mixing bowl, add the cooked onion and mix well until thoroughly blended. Be sure to season well.

To stuff the bird, season the turkey well with salt and pepper. Lay the tongue and strips of ham lengthwise inside the turkey then spread stuffing around the tongue and ham so that the bird takes on a turkey shape again. Secure any loose skin around the stuffing with skewers and truss the turkey with string around the legs and wings so that the turkey will keep its shape during cooking.

To cook, heat the oven to 350°F/180°C/Gas Mark 4. Stand the turkey in a large roasting tin. Season with salt and pepper and roast in the oven for 2½–3 hours. To test when the turkey is cooked, pierce the thigh with a fine skewer and if the juices that run out of the bird are clear then the turkey is cooked. If they are slightly tinged with pink then return to the oven for a further 15 minutes to finish cooking. Allow the turkey to become quite cold then remove the skewers and string. Chill in the refrigerator overnight then serve in slices with salad.

Serves about 20, more if there are a choice of meats

Ballotine of Duck

1 duckling about 4½lb (1.9kg)
watercress and slices of orange, to
  garnish

For the stuffing
1oz (25g) butter
1 tablespoon sunflower oil
1 medium onion, chopped
8oz (225g) pork sausagemeat
8oz (225g) raw pork, minced
4 chicken breasts, cut into strips
2 tablespoons freshly chopped
  parsley
½ teaspoon ground mace
salt
freshly ground black pepper
6 quails' eggs, hard-boiled for 3
  minutes

As ducks do not have a great abundance of meat, this is an excellent way of serving duck cold for a buffet as everyone is sure to have a good slice of meat. Remove the legs and wings just before carving as this makes for easier slicing. The legs and wings can then either be served with the slices of meat for the buffet or used in a soup or casserole.

Start by boning the duck. Lay the duck breast down, and with a very sharp small knife cut a slit down the back. Carefully pull the skin and flesh away from the carcass by scraping the knife along the carcass in short sharp strokes to release the flesh. Continue all around the rib cage releasing the leg and wing joints so that the whole of the rib cage can be lifted out of the duck. Leave the legs and wings in place as these will give the duck a better shape when cooked. Use the carcass bones for stock.

For the stuffing, heat the butter and oil in a pan and fry the onion for about 5 minutes until golden brown. Measure all the remaining ingredients except the eggs into a large mixing bowl, then add the fried onion. Season lightly and mix well until thoroughly blended.

Open out the duck and season well with salt and pepper. Spread half the stuffing over the duck and arrange the eggs in a row, end to end, down the middle, then place the remaining stuffing on top. Wrap the sides of the duck up over the stuffing so that it is back to its original 'bird' shape, and secure with skewers.

Stand the duck on a wire rack in a roasting tin and roast in the oven at 350°F/180°C/Gas Mark 4 for about 2 hours until tender. To test when the duck is cooked, pierce the thickest part of the thigh with a fine skewer; if clear juices run out then the duck is cooked. Allow to cool then remove the skewers, wrap in foil and chill in the refrigerator overnight before serving carved in slices, garnished with plenty of watercress and slices of orange.

Serves 12 with other meats

English Ham

I do admit that this recipe is a bit of a cheat, but when preparing a large buffet party it is a joy to have dishes that do not require lengthy preparation and cooking. This ham is a great time-saver and means you have extra time to spend on doing other things. Boneless carving hams are available from cash and carry's, and if local delicatessens are given plenty of warning then they will order one for you. The home-made glaze makes the ham look wonderful and being boneless there are no problems with carving. Decorate with cocktail cherries secured with cocktail sticks.

9–10lb (4–4.5kg) boneless
  carving ham

For the glaze
6oz (175g) demerara sugar
2 good tablespoons dry mustard

Heat the oven to 400°F/200°C/Gas Mark 6. Remove the ham from the plastic vacuum pack and gently peel off the skin, leaving as much fat as possible still on the ham.

For the glaze, mix the sugar and mustard in a bowl. Mark the fat on the ham into a diamond pattern with a sharp knife then press the glaze evenly on to the top fatty part of the ham. Wrap all the lean part of the ham in foil so that only the glazed part is showing. Lift the ham into a roasting tin and cook in the oven for about 15 minutes until the glaze is an even golden brown.

Remove from the oven and cool quickly then chill in the refrigerator before carving into slices to serve. Serve with Cumberland Sauce.

This size ham will serve at least 25 people, and even more if served with a choice of meats

Cumberland Sauce

2 oranges
2 lemons
8oz (225g) redcurrent jelly
¼ pint (150ml) port
about 3 heaped teaspoons
　　arrowroot
3 tablespoons cold water

This sauce for English Ham was a great success at my birthday party, and everyone wanted the recipe!

Thinly peel the rind from the oranges and lemons with a vegetable peeler. Squeeze out the juice from the fruit and strain into a pan. Add the redcurrant jelly to the fruit juices and heat gently until the jelly has melted.

Meanwhile shred the peel finely and place in a small pan, cover with cold water and bring to the boil. Strain and discard the water. Cover with fresh water, bring back to the boil, then cover with a lid and simmer for about 20 minutes until the peel is tender. Drain it thoroughly on kitchen paper.

Add the port to the jelly and bring to the boil, stirring constantly. Simmer for 2 minutes then remove from the heat. Blend the arrowroot with the water in a cup then sir into the jelly. Return to the heat, and bring back to the boil, stirring continuously until thickened. Stir in the peel. Allow to cool then pour into a serving jug. Cover with clingfilm and chill well in the refrigerator before serving.

Steak and Kidney Pie

2½lb (1.1kg) skirt beef
8oz (225g) ox kidney
3oz (75g) flour
2 tablespoons sunflower oil
1oz (25g) butter
2 large onions, chopped
2 pints (1.2 litres) good beef stock
salt
freshly ground black pepper
8oz (225g) mushrooms, sliced
1lb (450g) frozen puff pastry,
　　thawed
a little beaten egg, to glaze

This is always a great favourite, particularly with the men! Serve with creamy mashed potato and a green vegetable such as broccoli or French beans.

Cut the steak and kidney into 1 inch (2.5cm) pieces, put in a polythene bag with the flour and toss until well coated. Heat the oil and butter in a large pan, add the meat and fry with the onion until browned. Stir in the stock and seasoning and bring to the boil. Transfer to an ovenproof casserole dish and cook in the oven at 350°F/180°C/Gas Mark 4 for about 2½ hours, then stir in the mushrooms and continue cooking for a further 30 minutes or until the meat is tender. Taste to check seasoning, turn into a pie dish and allow to become cold.

Put a pie funnel or handle-less cup in the centre. Roll out the pastry on a lightly floured surface and use to cover the pie, seal and crimp the edges and use any pastry trimmings to decorate the top. Brush the pie with a little beaten egg and make a small hole in the centre for the steam to escape.

To serve, heat the oven to 425°F/220°C/Gas Mark 7, and bake the pie for 50 minutes. If the pastry is browning too much reduce the heat to 350°F/180°C/Gas Mark 4, and cook for a further 15 minutes until the pastry is golden brown and the meat has heated through.

Iced Lemon Flummery

For buffets, it's best to have the desserts in small individual dishes: this makes serving so much simpler as people can just help themselves. Make these ices days ahead, keep them in the freezer then, 10 minutes before serving, take them out and decorate.

½ pint (300 ml) double cream
grated rind and juice of 2 lemons
12oz (350g) caster sugar
1 pint (600 ml) milk

To serve
¼ pint (150 ml) whipping
   cream, whipped
a few sprigs of fresh mint or
   lemon balm

Pour the cream into a bowl and whisk until it forms soft peaks. Stir in the lemon rind, juice, sugar and milk and mix well until thoroughly blended. Pour into a 2½ pint (1.5 litre) plastic container, cover with a lid and freeze for at least 6 hours until firm. Cut into chunks and process in a processor or blender until smooth and creamy. Pour into twelve small ramekin dishes or chocolate pots and return to the freezer until required.

To serve, pipe a small blob of cream on top of each ramekin and decorate with a sprig of mint. The ramekins will keep perfectly for about 20 minutes or so before they start to melt.

Caramel Syllabub

This pudding is best prepared a short while before the party, if left too long the breadcrumbs begin to become soggy within the syllabub. But the breadcrumbs and syllabub can be separately prepared well ahead, and then just stirred together when required.

6oz (175g) fresh brown
   breadcrumbs
6oz (175g) muscovado sugar
1½ pints (900ml) double cream
grated rind and juice of 2 large
   lemons
3 tablespoons brandy
3 tablespoons sherry

Place the breadcrumbs and muscovado sugar on a piece of foil and toast under a hot grill until golden brown and caramelised, stirring occasionally. Keep a watchful eye whilst the crumbs are browning, and wait for them to turn a dark chestnut colour. This will take about 6 minutes or so. Leave to become cold.

For the syllabub, measure all the remaining ingredients into a bowl and whisk until light, but not thick.

To serve, stir the breadcrumbs into the syllabub and spoon into twelve tall serving glasses. Serve with brandy snaps or biscuits.

Gâteau Queen Victoria

A dark, spongy moist chocolate cake, best eaten with a fork. The gâteau can be made a day ahead and should then be stored in the refrigerator before serving.

For the cake
12 large eggs
10oz (275g) caster sugar
3oz (75g) cocoa, sieved
1oz (25g) self-raising flour

For the filling and sides
1 pint (600 ml) whipping cream,
 whipped
4oz (100g) flaked almonds,
 toasted

For the topping
4oz (100g) plain chocolate
4 tablespoons water
1oz (25g) butter
6oz (175g) icing sugar, sieved
½ pint (300 ml) whipping
 cream, whipped

Heat the oven to 350°F/180°C/Gas Mark 4. Grease and line with greased greaseproof paper two 10 inch (25cm) round deep cake tins.

First separate the eggs, putting the whites in a large bowl and the yolks into a smaller bowl. Add the caster sugar, cocoa and flour to the yolks and whisk until thick. Whisk the whites with a small electric or rotary whisk until they form stiff peaks. Add 3 tablespoons of the whisked whites to the yolks. Mix together then add this yolk mixture to the whites. Fold in with a metal spoon until thoroughly blended. Divide between the tins, level out evenly and bake in the oven for about 35 minutes until beginning to shrink away from the sides of the tins. Leave to cool in the tins for 5 minutes then turn out, remove paper and finish cooling on wire racks. Do expect the cake to sink a little on cooling.

When cold, sandwich the cakes together with half the whipped cream and stand on a serving plate or stand. Spread the remaining cream evenly around the sides of the cake and sprinkle the almonds on to this so they evenly coat the sides of the cake.

For the topping, put the chocolate, water and butter in a bowl and heat gently over a pan of simmering water until the mixture has melted. Remove from the heat and beat in the icing sugar until smooth, then allow to cool but not set. Pipe the cream for the topping in large swirls around the outside of the cake then pour the chocolate topping into the middle, spread out evenly and leave to set.

Serves 12–16

SCOTTISH HIGHLAND BUFFET

The Scots love to celebrate occasions like Hogmanay (New Year's Eve to the Sassenachs) and Burns' Night (25th January, Robert Burns' birthday). Hallowe'en might be another Scottish celebration. All are cold-weather occasions, so call for warming food and generous measures of whisky!

The Scots are renowned for their good quality meat and, of course, their fresh salmon. Here are a few of my favourite recipes which make the best use of these and other foods, and which are ideal to serve for a buffet party. On the whole, Scottish dishes do not tend to be very elaborate and highly seasoned, but are cooked well and simply and served without fuss.

Whisky, of course, is a prerequisite of any Scottish celebration, and there are number of good whisky cocktails and punches (anathema, in fact, to the whisky purists). Another idea might be Atholl Brose (a pudding on page 101) served as a drink. Soak 3 tablespoons oatmeal for 30 minutes in 1 pint (600 ml) water, then strain carefully. Mix the water with 2 tablespoons runny honey and add whisky to taste (usually about the same again as the water). You could add some cream to make it even more smooth and delicious.

Menu

BURNS' NIGHT SUPPER FOR 12

A wonderful excuse for a party and bound to be a boozy one. Some Scots pour whisky on the haggis as well as drink it most of the evening!

Haggis with bashed neeps

Pheasant in Cider

Sheila's Layered Vegetables

Scalloped Potatoes
(page 60)

Burnt Cream

Whisky Trifle

Preparation Hints

Haggis

Buy about 2lb (900g) haggis, boil it for about 30 minutes or as instructed. Slice into twelve slices and arrange on an oval dish surrounded with 3lb (1.4kg) mashed swedes, adding lots of black pepper and butter. Serve with whisky.

Pheasant in Cider

Cook the pheasant the day before, then reheat on the day.

Vegetables

Prepare both dishes the day ahead, and bake on the day.

Puddings

Make the Whisky Trifle the day before. Make the custard part of the Burnt Cream the day before, then do the caramel about 3 hours before serving, then chill.

Menu

NEW YEAR'S EVE BUFFET (HOT) FOR 24

2 × Buchanan Herrings

2 × Venison Casserole

2 × Scots Stovies

Buttered broccoli

Atholl Brose

Whisky Trifle

Cheese and biscuits

Preparation Hints

Buchanan Herrings

This starter just needs to be assembled on the day.

Venison Casserole

Can be cooked in advance and reheated.

Scots Stovies

This recipe contains lamb, but for this occasion leave the lamb out. You only want the soft stewed potatoes to accompany the venison.

Atholl Brose

Because it is so simple to make, make on the day; just buy the ingredients the day before.

Cheese and biscuits

There are quite a few interesting Scottish cheeses, and you could serve them with bought or home-made oatcakes.

NEW YEAR'S EVE BUFFET (COLD) FOR 12

Scotch Broth

Salmon with Cucumber Mayonnaise

Selection of salads

Baked Potatoes *(page 59)*

Edinburgh Tart

Preparation Hints

Scotch Broth

Make the day before, slightly *under*-cooking it. Chill and re-heat just before serving.

Salmon and Cucumber Mayonnaise

Can be made a day ahead and kept in the fridge, though it is slightly better when made on the day. The mayonnaise can be made ahead, of course.

Salads

Make them up on the day; the dressings can be made ahead.

Edinburgh Tart

Can be made the day before. Best served warm with lashings of cream. If you want, add some whisky to the whipped double cream.

Scotch Broth

I like to serve this warming soup for a buffet when I am serving light cold meats and salads as the main course.

Soak the barley, peas and lentils in a bowl of water overnight.

Trim excess fat off the lamb and discard. Put the lamb in a large pan with the water and seasoning and stir in the strained dried vegetables. Bring to the boil, cover with a lid and simmer for about an hour then add the freshly chopped vegetables and cook for a further hour. Lift the lamb out of the pan, break off all the meat, cut it into small pieces and return to the pan. Discard the bones. Taste and check seasoning then serve piping hot, sprinkled with a little freshly chopped parsley.

1½oz (40g) pearl barley
1oz (25g) dried peas
1oz (25g) dried lentils
1½lb (675g) scrag end neck of lamb, jointed
4 pints (2.25 litres) water
about 2 teaspoons salt
freshly ground black pepper
1lb (450g) chopped fresh vegetables (onion, leek and carrots)

To serve
a little freshly chopped parsley

Buchanan Herrings

One of the most delicious and simple first courses. It's quite an unusual combination, the banana taking away the sharpness of the rollmop herrings. Use a good brand of thick mayonnaise – or make your own. Serve with brown bread and butter.

Peel the bananas, cut each in half lengthways then slice into a bowl. Pour over lemon juice and blend together then stir in the mayonnaise. Cut the rollmops into small manageable pieces and stir into the mayonnaise.

Arrange the green salad over twelve individual small plates, then divide the herring mixture between them. Decorate with parsley, dill or fennel.

6 bananas
juice of 1 lemon
½ pint (300 ml) thick real mayonnaise (page 41)
4 rollmop herrings
enough mixed green salad to cover 12 plates
fresh parsley, dill or fennel

Salmon with Cucumber Mayonnaise

12 salmon steaks
4oz (100g) butter
juice of 1 lemon
salt
freshly ground black pepper

For the topping
½ cucumber, very finely sliced
½ pint (300 ml) aspic
2 tablespoons freshly chopped
  parsley

For the mayonnaise
1 pint (600 ml) mayonnaise
  (page 41)
½ cucumber, chopped
juice of 1 lemon

This salmon dish really is very simple indeed but quite delicious.

Heat the oven to 375°F/190°C/Gas Mark 5.

Butter a large shallow ovenproof dish well, and lay the salmon steaks in it so they are just touching. Dot each of the steaks with a knob of the butter and sprinkle with lemon juice and salt and pepper. Bake in the oven for about 20 minutes until the fish is pink and opaque. Allow to cool then lift on to a large serving platter. Chill in the refrigerator for a couple of hours so the aspic will set more quickly.

Toss the cucumber slices and parsley in the aspic and arrange on top of each of the salmon steaks; because they've been chilled, the aspic should set on touching the salmon. Spoon any remaining aspic on top. To serve, garnish with a little fresh parsley or dill.

For the mayonnaise, mix all the ingredients in a bowl, turn into a serving dish and serve separately with the salmon steaks.

Scottish Brisket of Beef

4½–5lb (2kg–2.25kg) salted
  brisket of beef, boned
2 onions, roughly chopped
8 cloves
4 bay leaves
2 carrots, sliced
4 sticks of celery, chopped
10 black peppercorns

Do chill the joint overnight as this makes for easier carving. Serve with a selection of salads.

Put the brisket in a pan just large enough to take it. Add the remaining ingredients and just enough water to cover it. Slowly bring to the boil and lift off any scum with a spoon. Cover with a lid and simmer very gently for about 3½–4 hours until the meat is very tender. Top up with water if necessary during cooking.

Lift the joint out of the pan, remove any peppercorns etc which may be sticking to it and cut off surplus fat. Place in a cake tin which is just a little too small for it, cover with a plate and weigh down with weights. Leave to become cold then chill in the refrigerator overnight.

To serve, turn out of the tin with care and cut downwards into thin slices.

Venison Casserole

Venison is farmed in the highlands of Scotland and is eaten far more frequently than we eat it in England. It does have a flavour all of its own and I find it best to give it a long slow cook to tenderise the meat. This recipe is one I often use for supper parties.

Heat the oven to 325°F/160°C/Gas Mark 3.

Heat the butter and oil in a large pan and quickly fry the meat until browned. Lift out with a slotted spoon and place in a large ovenproof dish. Add the onion to the juices remaining in the pan and cook for about 5 minutes until soft, then add the mushrooms and cook for a further 2 minutes. Stir in the flour and gradually blend in the cider. Bring to the boil, stirring until thickened, then add the stock cubes, salt, pepper and nutmeg. Pour over the venison, cover with a lid or piece of foil and cook in the oven for between 2 and 3 hours until the venison is tender. Taste and check seasoning.

Sprinkle with chopped parsley and serve with mashed potato and a fresh green vegetable.

2oz (50g) butter
2 tablespoons sunflower oil
4lb (1.8kg) stewing venison, cut into neat cubes
6 large onions, sliced
12oz (350g) button mushrooms
1 tablespoon flour
1½ pints (900 ml) cider
4 beef stock cubes, crumbled
salt
freshly ground black pepper
½ teaspoon ground nutmeg
freshly chopped parsley to garnish

Pheasant in Cider

Do remember that the cooking time of pheasants will very according to the age of the birds. This dish can be prepared well ahead and kept in the refrigerator until required then reheated until piping hot.

Heat the oven to 350°F/180°C/Gas Mark 4.

Heat 2 tablespoons of the oil in a pan and fry the pheasants one at a time until lightly browned all over. Arrange in a large ovenproof dish. Add the bacon, onion, mushrooms and garlic to the juices remaining in the pan and fry for about 10 minutes before spooning over the pheasants.

Heat the remaining oil and fry the apple slices until just tender. Stir in flour then gradually blend in the cider. Bring to the boil, stirring until thickened. Season well with salt and pepper and pour over the pheasants. Cover the dish with a lid or piece of foil and cook in the oven for about 1½ hours or until the pheasants are tender.

Lift the pheasants out of the casserole and carve off the leg and breast portions. Discard the ends of the wings and the carcass and use for stock. Return the portions to the casserole. Taste and check seasoning, reheat in the oven and serve sprinkled with freshly chopped parsley.

4 tablespoons sunflower oil
2 brace pheasants
4oz (100g) streaky bacon finely chopped
2 large onions, sliced
6oz (175g) button mushrooms
2 fat cloves of garlic, crushed
2lb (900g) Bramley apples, peeled, cored and sliced
2 good tablespoons flour
1½ pints (900 ml) cider
salt
freshly ground black pepper
freshly chopped parsley, to serve

Scots Stovies

2lb (900g) cooked lamb
3lb (1.4kg) potatoes, sliced
3 large onions, sliced
salt
freshly ground black pepper
1 pint (600 ml) good stock
a little freshly chopped parsley,
    to serve

This dish should ideally be made in a large shallow pan on top of the stove but since for a buffet there are likely to be a lot of guests then it is easiest to cook it in the oven. This will brown the potatoes on top too.

Heat the oven to 350°F/180°C/Gas Mark 4. Finely chop the lamb, and arrange in layers with the potatoes and onions in a large shallow oven-proof dish, seasoning well between each layer. Finish with a layer of potatoes on top. Pour over the stock, cover with a piece of foil and bake in the oven for an hour then remove the foil and cook for about a further 45 minutes or until the vegetables are tender and the potatoes on top have browned.

Serve hot, sprinkled with a little freshly chopped parsley with peas or beans to give a bit of colour.

Sheila's Layered Vegetables

1oz (25g) butter
1 tablespoon sunflower oil
3 large onions, chopped
2½lb (1.2kg) tomatoes, skinned
    and sliced
2 teaspoons sugar
salt
freshly ground black pepper
2lb (900g) courgettes, thinly
    sliced
1 large red pepper, skinned and
    cut into thin strips
4oz (100g) fresh white
    breadcrumbs
a little oil

This is a delicious combination of vegetables which takes only a short while to prepare. I find it is best to layer the vegetables up fairly thickly rather than spreading them out in a shallow dish and then they retain their moisture during cooking.

Heat the oven to 350°F/180°C/Gas Mark 4.

Heat the butter and oil in a pan and gently fry the onion for about 10 minutes until beginning to soften. Spread thickly in the bottom of an ovenproof dish then layer the tomatoes on top. Sprinkle with the sugar and season well with salt and pepper. Arrange the courgettes on top of the tomatoes and use the strips of skinned red pepper to form a lattice over the top of the vegetables. Sprinkle with the breadcrumbs, brush lightly with oil and bake in the oven for about 45 minutes until the vegetables are just tender and the breadcrumbs are golden brown.

Serve straight from the oven.

Burnt Cream

This dessert is sheer luxury, and is not difficult to make at all. Burnt Cream is the Scottish name for Crême Brûlée. Choose a large, shallow dish that will withstand being put under the grill. Make the cream custard part a day ahead, then put the sugar topping on three hours before serving.

8 egg yolks
2oz (50g) caster or vanilla sugar
2 pints (1.2 litres) single cream
about 4oz (100g) demerara sugar

Heat the oven to 325°F/160°C/Gas Mark 3. Butter well a shallow 3 pint (1.75 litre) ovenproof dish or 12 small ramekin dishes.

Beat the egg yolks with the caster or vanilla sugar. (If you haven't any vanilla sugar but like the flavour, then add a little vanilla essence.) Heat the cream to scalding and gradually beat in the egg yolks mixture. Pour the mixture into the dish or dishes, stand in a baking tin half filled with warm water, and cook in the oven for about 55 minutes or until set. If using small dishes, they will need only 30–35 minutes cooking time. Take out of the oven and leave to cool.

Sprinkle the top thickly with demerara sugar and put under a hot grill. Watch carefully until the sugar melts and then caramelises to a golden brown. Remove from the grill and chill well for about 3 hours before serving.

Atholl Brose

If preparing a Scottish buffet, this is a must to serve as the dessert. It should be prepared just before serving, but really doesn't take any time at all if you have all the ingredients out ready to put together. Traditionally you should add toasted porridge oats but I prefer to omit them.

1 pint (600 ml) double cream
1 pint (600 ml) natural yoghurt
8 tablespoons runny honey
about 6 tablespoons whisky, to
  taste

Whisk the cream in a bowl until it forms soft peaks then gently fold in the yoghurt and honey. Stir in the whisky, taste then add a little more if necessary.

Divide between twelve tall stemmed glasses and serve with thin crisp biscuits or brandy snaps.

Whisky Trifle

2 packets of trifle sponges (each
   with 8 sponges)
strawberry jam
4 macaroons, broken up
1lb (450g) can of pear halves,
   drained and juice reserved
6 tablespoons Scotch whisky

For the custard
6 egg yolks
2oz (50g) caster sugar
2 heaped teaspoons cornflour
1 pint (600 ml) milk

Topping
½ pint (300 ml) whipping
   cream, whipped
2oz (50g) flaked almonds,
   toasted
5 strawberries (optional)

Scotland is, of course, the home of whisky and I could not possibly have missed out a recipe including whisky in this section.

Split the sponges, spread with strawberry jam and sandwich together. Cut each sponge into six small squares and use to line the bottom of a shallow 12 inch (30cm) glass serving dish. Scatter over the crumbled macaroons, then arrange the pears on top. Mix the whisky with the reserved pear juice, pour over the sponges, then press down firmly to give an even surface.

For the custard, mix together the egg yolks, sugar and cornflour. Heat the milk in a pan until almost boiling then pour on to the egg yolks, mix well then return to the pan. Heat gently, stirring until thickened. Allow to cool then whisk for a few moments until light, then pour over the trifle. Allow to set completely then top with the whipped cream and decorate with the toasted almonds and halved strawberries if liked. Chill really well before serving.

Edinburgh Tart

For the pastry
8oz (225g) plain flour
5oz (150g) margarine
about 3 tablespoons cold water to
   mix

For the filling
4oz (100g) butter
4oz (100g) caster sugar
4oz (100g) raisins
2oz (50g) glacé cherries, halved
4oz (100g) chopped mixed peel
2 tablespoons whisky
3 eggs, beaten

My cousin who lives in Scotland first introduced me to this recipe. It is very rich but delicious. Heat a baking tray in the oven whilst the oven is heating up as this ensures that the tart pastry will be cooked underneath.

Heat the oven to 400°F/200°C/Gas Mark 6.

For the pastry measure the flour into a bowl and rub in the margarine until the mixture resembles fine breadcrumbs. Add sufficient water to form a firm dough and knead gently until smooth. Roll out on a lightly floured surface and use to line a 9 inch (22.5cm) loose-bottomed fluted flan tin. Save all the pastry trimmings.

For the filling, melt the butter in a pan, add the sugar and heat gently until the sugar has dissolved. Remove from the heat, stir in the remaining ingredients, and pour into the prepared pastry case. Re-roll the pastry trimmings, cut into strips and use to make a lattice on top of the flan. Bake in the oven for about 30 minutes until the pastry is golden brown and the filling has set.

AMERICAN BUFFET

Americans entertain lavishly and generously and splendidly, and pay great attention to even the smallest detail. I shall never forget the party given by a very glamorous American hostess (the one who gave me the Chicken Divan recipe) at her summer house in the country: it was the nearest I shall probably get to a *Dynasty* setting. The weather was glorious, the tables were covered in pink clothes and bowls of Icelandic poppies, and the food was quite delicious, all prepared with a minimum of fuss.

The 4th of July, Independence Day, is a major time of celebration, but another is Thanksgiving, on the fourth Thursday in November. Traditionally hot turkey is served, and it can be fun to have turkey before Christmas. American stuffings are often sweeter than ours: perhaps cranberries and rice, or an apricot, nut and onion stuffing. Sometimes the turkey is served with sweet potatoes, but it is almost always followed by a pumpkin pie to echo the first meal allegedly enjoyed by the Pilgrim Fathers when they finally reached America.

If giving an American buffet, you can go to town with the puddings. The Americans are particularly lavish with their icecreams. Layer up different flavoured icecreams, fruits, syrups, and lashings of cream. Decorate with mini marshmallows, mint chocolates, or buy paper cocktail umbrellas and sparklers to finish off these flamboyant puddings in true American style.

A summer party could be preceded by any of the vast selection of American cocktails, but always remember to serve masses of crushed ice for authenticity! A julep with mint would be very appropriate for the Southern Country Buffet: a simple combination of bourbon or Scotch whisky, a little sugar, lots of mint sprigs and crushed ice. Serve a Californian wine with the meal if you can.

Menu

SOUTHERN COUNTRY BUFFET FOR 12

Turkey Jambalaya or American Beefburgers

American Iceberg Salad or Waldorf Salad

New York Potatoes

Pecan Pie

Grapefruit Mousse

Preparation Hints

*If you want a starter, Avocado Mousse is delicious – but more bother
for the hostess! You might like to serve it before the American Beefburgers.*

Turkey Jambalaya

The American answer to
risotto. Cook it ahead, as it
reheats well.

American Beefburgers

Can be prepared well in
advance, covered with
clingfilm and left in the
fridge. Don't grill them for
too long as it is nice to have
them pink in the middle.

Salads

The dressings can be prepared
well in advance.

New York Potatoes

Can be scraped a day ahead
and kept in a cool place. Cook
them an hour or so before you
need them, and they will keep
hot for up to an hour in a cool
oven.

Pecan Pie

Exceedingly sweet and very
traditional. Pecans are very
expensive and I find that I can
get away with using walnuts
in the pie itself and just using
the pecans for decoration.

Grapefruit Mousse

The tartness of this
counteracts the sweetness of
the pie.

Menu

4th JULY HOLIDAY BUFFET FOR 12

Chicken Divan

Tossed Green Salad
(page 39)

Wholewheat Bread
(page 42)

Icecream Bar

or

Refrigerator Cheesecake

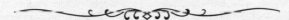

Preparation Hints

Chicken Divan

Best if it is not kept hot for too long.

Salad

Prepare and toss shortly before serving.

Wholewheat Bread

Can be made well in advance.

Icecream Bar

Good American icecream is available in many places, but if you cannot find it, serve a selection of good British icecreams. Arrange them on a table or 'bar' with bowls of fresh fruit, toppings and sauces. Strawberries, sliced bananas, cherries, raspberries, toasted almonds, broken-up peanut brittle, broken-up mint rock, chocolate sauces, Melba sauce, fudge sauce in small jugs. You stand behind the bar and have glasses and dishes ready – and take your orders. This is particularly good for teenagers' parties: put the menu up showing the various types on order, perhaps even draw pictures of them – peach melba, banana-split, etc. Have a choice of three.

Have a selection of small biscuits to go with the icecream, such as langues de chat and twiles (little almond biscuits) and brandy snaps – all bought of course.

Refrigerator Cheesecake

This can be made well in advance.

Avocado Mousse

½oz (15g) gelatine
3 tablespoons cold water
¼ pint (150 ml) good chicken
stock
3 ripe avocado pears
salt
freshly ground black pepper
2 fat cloves of garlic, crushed
juice of ½ lemon
½ pint (300 ml) good thick
mayonnaise (page 41)
¼ pint (150 ml) double cream,
lightly whipped
1 curly endive, broken into small
pieces
a few whole prawns for
decoration

This mousse looks very pretty when it is turned out, with the avocado peeping out from the mousse mixture. Serve with salad and crusty brown rolls and butter as a first course. For more special occasions, fill the centre of the ring mould with a prawn mixture. Blend ½ pint (300 ml) mayonnaise with 3 teaspoons tomato purée, the juice of a ½ lemon, a little Worcestershire sauce and lots of black pepper. Mix in 12oz (350g) well drained shelled prawns.

Put the gelatine in a bowl with the cold water and leave to stand for about 3 minutes to form a sponge, then stand over a bowl of simmering water until dissolved. Allow to cool then stir into the stock.

Peel and quarter one of the avocados, removing the stone, and place the flesh in a processor or blender with the stock, salt, pepper, garlic and lemon juice. Reduce to a smooth purée then gently fold in the mayonnaise and cream.

Lightly oil a 2½ pint (1.5 litre) ring mould. Peel the other two avocados, cut in half and remove the stones. Place them in the ring mould, with their cut surfaces facing upwards. Pour the mousse mixture around the avocados to fill the mould. Leave in the fridge to set.

To serve, arrange the endive on a serving plate and turn the mousse out on to this. Decorate with a few whole prawns and serve in slices with more salad.

American Beefburgers

2lb (900g) best quality minced
beef
1lb (450g) beef sausagemeat
1 large onion, grated
salt
freshly ground black pepper
a little flour

These should be prepared from the best quality minced beef. If you know that the meat is of particularly good quality, then they can be cooked so that they are still pink in the centre but brown and crisp on the outside.

Measure the mince, sausagemeat, onion, salt and pepper into a bowl and mix well until thoroughly blended. Cover with clingfilm and chill the mixture for about 3 hours so it is easier to handle.

Divide the mixture into twelve equal pieces and shape into chunky beefburgers with lightly floured hands. Chill again in the refrigerator for a couple of hours before cooking.

Arrange the beefburgers on a grill pan and cook under a hot grill for about 5 minutes on each side depending on how well cooked you like them. Serve in warm baps with lots of salad, corn relish and dill pickles.

American Chicken and Rice Salad

Tastes even better the day after it is made as then the flavours have had plenty of time to develop.

Measure all the ingredients into a large mixing bowl and toss lightly until thoroughly mixed. Turn into a large serving dish. Cover with clingfilm and chill in the refrigerator until required (preferably overnight).

Serves 12 with a choice of other salads

12oz (350g) long-grain
   American rice, cooked
1/2 pint (300 ml) good thick
   mayonnaise (page 41)
2 dessertspoons runny honey
grated rind and juice of 2 small
   lemons
10 spring onions, chopped
1 1/2lb (675g) cooked diced
   chicken
15oz (427g) can of pineapple
   chunks, drained
salt
freshly ground black pepper

Chicken Divan

This recipe is quick and easy to prepare and very delicious. It can be prepared well in advance and then reheated as required. Do not reheat for longer otherwise the sauce will curdle.

Heat the oven to 350°F/180°C/Gas Mark 4.

Heat the butter and oil in a pan and quickly fry the chicken breasts until browned all over. Lift out with a slotted spoon and arrange in the bottom of a large ovenproof dish. Arrange the broccoli spears around the chicken. Empty the contents of the cans of soup into a large bowl and add the cream, mayonnaise, lemon juice, curry powder, salt and pepper and mix well. Spoon over the top of the chicken. Sprinkle with the grated cheeses and then a little paprika pepper, and cook in the oven for about 40 minutes until the sauce is bubbling and the chicken is tender.

Serve with granary rolls and a tossed green salad.

2oz (50g) butter
1 tablespoon sunflower oil
12 chicken breasts, skinned and
   boned
1lb (450g) frozen broccoli
   spears, thawed
2 × 10.6oz (300g) cans of
   condensed chicken soup
1/2 pint (300 ml) soured cream
1/2 pint (300 ml) mayonnaise
   (page 41)
juice of 1 lemon
1 teaspoon curry powder
salt and black pepper
8oz (225g) well flavoured
   Cheddar cheese, grated
2oz (50g) Parmesan cheese,
   grated
a little paprika pepper

Turkey Jambalaya

6oz (175g) flour
salt
freshly ground black pepper
cayenne pepper
3lb (1.4kg) casserole turkey
  meat, cubed
3oz (75g) bacon fat or lard
3 large onions, chopped
4 cloves of garlic, crushed
1 large red pepper, seeded and
  chopped
5 sticks of celery, chopped
8oz (225g) button mushrooms,
  sliced
1½lb (675g) long-grain rice
3 pints (1.75 litres) chicken stock

To serve
freshly chopped parsley

Jambalaya is traditionally a South American dish. I like to serve it with a dressed green salad. If turkey is difficult to get hold of then try pork or chicken instead. Both give excellent results.

Generously season the flour with salt, black and cayenne pepper. Toss the turkey meat in the flour until evenly coated. Heat the fat in a very large pan and quickly fry the meat until browned on all sides. Lift the turkey out of the pan with a slotted spoon and keep on one side.

Add the onions and garlic to the remaining fat in the pan and fry for about 10 minutes until beginning to brown. Stir in the red pepper, celery and mushrooms with the rice and cook for 2 minutes, stirring continuously, then add the stock, turkey and seasoning and bring to the boil. Cover with a lid and simmer gently, stirring occasionally, for about 40 minutes until all the liquid has been absorbed and the turkey is tender. Taste and check seasoning. Turn into a warm serving dish and serve sprinkled with freshly chopped parsley.

Waldorf Salad

1 small head of celery, broken
  into sticks and chopped
8 dessert apples, quartered, cored
  and diced
½ pint (300 ml) good thick
  mayonnaise (page 41)
¼ pint (150 ml) whipping
  cream, whipped
juice of ½ lemon
salt
freshly ground black pepper
6oz (175g) walnut pieces

If you are using ordinary green dessert apples then I would be inclined to peel them but if they are a pretty red colour then I would leave the peel on. Roughly chopped hard-boiled eggs may be added too, if liked.

Blend the celery, apple, mayonnaise, cream and lemon juice together in a bowl, season to taste, then chill in the refrigerator until required.

Just before serving stir in the walnut pieces. Turn into a serving bowl and serve with a choice of other salads.

American Iceberg Salad

The salad and dressing can be made well in advance. Iceburg lettuce is wonderful in that it stays crisp much longer than other lettuce.

Shred the lettuce and put in a large salad bowl with the watercress, which can be broken into small sprigs. Add the mushrooms, courgettes, spring onions and red pepper and toss well. Cover with clingfilm and leave until required.

For the dressing, blend all the ingredients together in a bowl and chill in the refrigerator until required. Serve the dressing in a small bowl along with the salad.

1 medium iceberg lettuce
2 bunches of watercress
3oz (75g) button mushrooms, sliced
2 courgettes, sliced
1 bunch of spring onions, chopped
1 red pepper, seeded and diced

For the dressing
¼ pint (150 ml) mayonnaise (page 41)
¼ pint (150 ml) soured cream
¼ pint (150 ml) natural yoghurt
4 tablespoons white wine vinegar
salt
freshly ground black pepper
2 fat cloves of garlic, crushed

New York Potatoes

I prefer to use baby new potatoes for this recipe, but when they are not available use larger potatoes cut into small pieces.

Heat the oven to 375°F/190°C/Gas Mark 5.

Dry the potatoes thoroughly. Put the butter in a large shallow ovenproof dish and heat in the oven until melted. Add the potatoes and roll in the butter until evenly coated, then add the cloves of garlic and season well. Cover with foil and cook in the oven for about an hour, shaking the dish occasionally until the potatoes are evenly coated with butter.

Remove the foil and return to the oven for a further 40 minutes or until the potatoes are tender. Remove the garlic cloves. Turn into a warm serving dish and pour over any butter left in the dish. Sprinkle with the chopped chives and parsley.

3lb (1.4kg) baby new potatoes, scraped
4oz (100g) butter
6 fat cloves of garlic, peeled
salt
freshly ground black pepper
about 2 tablespoons mixed chopped parsley and chives

Thousand Island Dressing

½ pint (300 ml) good
  mayonnaise (page 41)
¼ pint (150 ml) tomato ketchup
2oz (50g) stuffed olives, very
  finely chopped
1 small green pepper, seeded and
  chopped
2 tablespoons freshly snipped
  chives
2 hard-boiled eggs, chopped
salt
freshly ground black pepper

A very versatile American salad dressing, good to serve with iceburg lettuce, eggs, shellfish and open sandwiches.

Measure all the ingredients into a mixing bowl and blend thoroughly with a wooden spoon. Taste to check seasoning, then cover with clingfilm and chill in the refrigerator until required.

Will serve up to 12 as an accompaniment to salads

Pecan Pie

8oz (225g) plain flour
4oz (100g) butter
2oz (50g) lard
2 egg yolks
1oz (25g) caster sugar
about 2 teaspoons water

For the filling
2oz (50g) butter
12oz (350g) dark muscovado
  sugar
6 eggs
1lb (450g) maple syrup
2 teaspoons vanilla essence
½ teaspoon salt
6oz (175g) pecan nuts, halved

If you are unable to get maple syrup then use 10oz (275g) golden syrup with 2 tablespoons black treacle, and made up to 1lb (450g) with boiling water. Expect the filling to be very sweet – it is traditional!

To make the pastry, measure the flour into a bowl and rub in the fats until the mixture resembles fine breadcrumbs. Mix the yolks, sugar and water together and work into the dry ingredients to form a firm dough. Wrap in clingfilm and chill in the refrigerator for about 30 minutes. Meanwhile, heat the oven to 425°F/220°C/Gas Mark 7.

Roll out the pastry on a lightly floured surface and use to line a deep 10 inch (25cm) loose-bottomed flan tin. Line with greaseproof paper and baking beans or a piece of foil and bake blind in the oven for about 10 minutes then remove the paper and beans or the foil and return to the oven for a further 5 minutes.

For the filling, cream the butter and sugar together, whisk the eggs and add to the creamed mixture with the maple syrup, vanilla essence and salt. Beat well. Arrange the nuts over the base of the flan flat side down. Pour in the filling and bake in the oven turned down to 375°F/190°C/Gas Mark 5 for about 50–60 minutes. The pie will sink a little as it cools. Serve warm in wedges with cream.

Refrigerator Cheesecake

This cheesecake has a wonderful texture, really light and creamy. It can be prepared well ahead and then decorated just before serving.

8oz (225g) digestive biscuits, crushed
½ teaspoon cinnamon
½ teaspoon grated nutmeg
3oz (75g) butter, melted

First make the crust. Lightly grease a 10 inch (25cm) round, deep loose-bottomed cake tin. Mix the biscuit crumbs, cinnamon, nutmeg and butter together in a bowl until thoroughly blended then turn into the prepared tin and level out evenly with the back of a metal spoon to cover the base.

For the filling
½ oz (15g) gelatine
5 tablespoons water
4 eggs, separated
3oz (75g) caster sugar
½ pint (300 ml) whipping cream, whipped
1lb (450g) rich cream cheese
grated rind and juice of 2 lemons

For the filling measure the gelatine and water into a bowl and leave to stand for about 3 minutes to form a sponge. Stand the bowl over a pan of simmering water until the gelatine has dissolved. Beat the egg yolks and sugar together in a bowl until creamy and light in colour then fold in the cooled, but not set, gelatine and the whipped cream. Beat the cream cheese, lemon rind and juice until smooth then fold into the yolk mixture. Whisk the egg whites with an electric or rotary whisk until they form stiff peaks then fold into the mixture until thoroughly blended. Pour this mixture over the prepared base, level out evenly and chill in the refrigerator for at least 4 hours until set. Just before serving, decorate with blobs of whipped cream and sprigs of fresh mint. Serve in slim wedges.

To decorate
¼ pint (150 ml) whipping cream, whipped
a few sprigs of fresh mint

Grapefruit Mousse

Light, refreshing and tangy.

8 eggs, separated
8oz (225g) caster sugar
2 large grapefruit
1oz (25g) gelatine
6 tablespoons cold water

Place the egg yolks in a bowl with the sugar and beat until creamy. Grate the rind from one of the grapefruit, squeeze the juice from both, and add rind and juice to the egg mixture.

Measure the gelatine into a small bowl with the cold water and allow to stand for about 3 minutes to form a sponge. Dissolve the gelatine over a pan of simmering water. Cool slightly then stir into the grapefruit mixture. Whisk the egg whites until stiff and fold into the grapefruit mixture. Turn carefully into a large glass serving bowl and chill until required. Serve with a crisp biscuit such as Anne Goss's Almond Biscuits (page 47), and you can decorate the mousse with cream if liked.

MEXICAN BUFFET

When testing and developing the recipes for this book, the Mexican Buffet was voted as one of the favourites by all concerned. The Picadillo is absolutely divine and we liked it best served in Tacos so it can easily be picked up and eaten in the fingers. The Guacamole and Bean Dip are good to serve with drinks in a bowl surrounded by Totopos for dunking. They can also be served in small individual bowls as a first course.

Mexicans are not great ones for serving rich elaborate puddings; it is more traditional to serve fresh fruits, a simple fruit salad or an icecream. As Mexico is the home of chocolate, they would also very likely serve fresh fruits – grapes, cherries and strawberries, etc – dipped in chocolate, a bit like we would serve *petits fours*.

To drink, you could serve tequila cocktails to start off with (Tequila Sunrise would be lovely, but it's so complicated to prepare), with a Mexican coffee or hot chocolate after dinner.

Menu

FINGER FOOD BUFFET FOR 24

2 × Bean Dip

2 × Guacamole

4 × Totopos

2 × Tacos and Picadillo

2 × Tostadas

Chocolate Fresh Fruits
(page 46)

Preparation Hints

Bean Dip

Prepare the day before, cover and keep in the fridge until required.

Totopos

Prepare ahead, but bake freshly to serve.

Guacamole

Prepare on the day.

Tacos and Picadillo

Make the Picadillo 1–2 days ahead and store in the fridge. Reheat and assemble Tacos to serve.

Tostadas

Prepare ingredients ahead and assemble to serve.

Chocolate Fresh Fruits

Prepare on the day.

Menu

FORK BUFFET FOR 12

Chilled Avocado with Melon and Prawns

Empanadas

1 Moctezuma Pie

Garlic Bread
(page 142)

Green Salad with Fennel
(page 39)

Mango Icecream

Chocolate Fresh Fruits
(page 46)

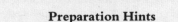

Preparation Hints

Chilled Avocado with Melon and Prawns

Prepare on the day itself, and assemble just before serving.

Empanadas

Make in advance and reheat as required.

Moctezuma Pie

Can be prepared the day before to baking stage, then covered and kept in the fridge. Bake to serve.

Garlic Bread

Prepare in advance, freeze even, and reheat to serve.

Green Salad with Fennel

Prepare on the day.

Mango Icecream

Can be made a few weeks ahead and stored in the freezer.

Chocolate Fresh Fruits

Prepare on the day.

Guacamole

A delicious light dip for a buffet table, to be served in a bowl surrounded by Totopos (page 117).

Mix the tomato, coriander, spring onions and seasoning together in a bowl. Just before serving, cut the avocados in half, remove the stones and scoop the flesh out on to a plate. Mash down with a fork and mix with the lemon juice, sugar and oil. Stir into the tomato mixture. Taste and check seasoning and turn into a bowl to serve.

8 firm tomatoes, skinned and chopped
1 teaspoon coriander seeds, crushed
6 spring onions, chopped
salt
freshly ground black pepper
2 large ripe avocados
juice of 1 lemon
4 teaspoons caster sugar
6 tablespoons sunflower oil

Chilled Avocado with Melon and Prawns

Ideally, this starter should be assembled just before serving, otherwise the melon will make the soured cream sauce too runny. Have all the ingredients prepared separately in the fridge just ready to put together at the last minute, it won't take long.

Cut the melon in half, scoop out and discard the seeds, then scoop out the flesh with a small melon baller and put in a bowl with the prawns, soured cream, salt, pepper, curry powder and mango chutney juice. Mix together well until thoroughly blended.

Cut the avocados in half and remove the stones, then arrange in halves in individual serving dishes. Brush the flesh with a little lemon juice to prevent it discolouring. Spoon the melon mixture on to the pears and serve straightaway decorated with a sprig of mint.

1 small ripe Gallia melon
12oz (350g) peeled prawns, well drained
1 pint (600 ml) soured cream
salt
freshly ground black pepper
1 teaspoon curry powder
2 tablespoons mango chutney juice
6 ripe avocado pears
juice of ½ lemon
12 sprigs of fresh mint

Bean Dip

1oz (25g) butter
1 tablespoon sunflower oil
1 large onion, chopped
14oz (397g) can of tomatoes
2 tablespoons tomato purée
1 tablespoon caster sugar
8oz (225g) Refried Beans
  (page 120)
4oz (100g) well flavoured
  Cheddar cheese, grated
salt
freshly ground black pepper

Again, this dip can be served in a bowl surrounded by Totopos or a selection of fresh vegetables crudités such as carrot, celery and cucumber sticks, florets of cauliflower or pieces of chicory.

Heat the butter and oil in a pan and gently fry the onion for about 10 minutes until soft. Stir in the tomatoes, purée and sugar and simmer gently for about 10 minutes until thick and pulpy. Stir in the beans, cheese and seasoning and stir until the cheese has melted. Remove from the heat and taste and check seasoning then turn into a serving dish and allow to cool before serving.

Tostadas

12 tostadas (crisply fried corn
  tortillas)

For the topping
8oz (225g) Refried Beans
  (page 120)
½ small iceburg lettuce, finely
  shredded
3 chicken breasts, cooked and
  sliced
6 tomatoes, sliced
½ cucumber, sliced
1 small onion, thinly sliced
1 ripe avocado, peeled, stoned
  and sliced
salt
freshly ground black pepper
½ pint (300 ml) soured cream
4oz (100g) well flavoured
  Cheddar cheese, grated
12 dill pickles

I think the best way to describe these is as mini open sandwiches which are piled high with filling. They are a little tricky to eat but are quite delicious. Use any variety of salad ingredients you may have at hand to add variety.

Heat the oven to 350°F/180°C/Gas Mark 4.
    Arrange the tostadas on a baking tray and reheat in the oven for about 10 minutes. Whilst these are heating through, gently warm the Refried Beans in a non-stick pan. Spread each of the tostadas with a layer of refried beans then layer up the lettuce, chicken, tomatoes, cucumber, onion and avocado, seasoning well. Spoon a little soured cream over the top of each, sprinkle with cheese and top with a dill pickle. Serve straightaway with a paper napkin!

Totopos

It is possible to buy tortilla chips in bags from health-food shops and some deli-catessens. They can be served on their own as 'nibbles' to go with drinks or as an accompaniment to a dip.

6oz (175g) tortilla chips
3oz (75g) well flavoured
   Cheddar cheese
a little cayenne pepper

Heat the oven to 400°F/200°C/Gas Mark 6.

Lay the tortilla chips out evenly over a baking tray, sprinkle with the cheese and a little cayenne and bake in the oven for about 10 minutes until the cheese has melted and is beginning to turn golden brown. Serve in bowls whilst still warm with drinks, or arrange on a platter with a bowl of dip in the middle.

Chicken Mexicano

Do take care when preparing a recipe using chilli. There is a great deal of difference between chilli seasoning and chilli powder, the latter being much hotter.

3oz (75g) flour
salt
freshly ground black pepper
2 level teaspoons chilli seasoning
12 chicken breasts, skinned and
   boned
2oz (50g) butter
2 tablespoons sunflower oil
2 large onions, chopped
1 large green pepper, cored,
   seeded and sliced
2 × 14oz (425g) cans of
   tomatoes
1 pint (600 ml) good chicken
   stock
3 tablespoons tomato purée
3 tablespoons white wine vinegar
2oz (50g) stuffed green olives,
   sliced

Heat the oven to 350°F/180°C/Gas Mark 4.

Measure the flour, salt, pepper and chilli seasoning on to a plate and mix well. Coat the breasts thoroughly in this. Heat the butter and oil in a pan and quickly fry the chicken until golden brown on all sides. Lift out with a slotted spoon and arrange in a large ovenproof dish. (It may be necessary to do the frying in batches.) Add the onions and pepper to the juices left in the pan and fry for about 5 minutes until soft. Stir in any remaining seasoned flour and cook for a minute. Gradually blend in the contents of the cans of tomatoes, the stock, purée and vinegar and bring to the boil, stirring until thickened. Remove from the heat, taste and check seasoning and pour over the chicken breasts.

Cover with a lid or piece of foil and bake in the oven for about 40 minutes until the chicken is tender and the sauce is bubbling. Sprinkle with the stuffed olives and serve hot with plain boiled rice and a green salad.

Moctezuma Pie

2oz (50g) butter
1 tablespoon sunflower oil
2 large onions, chopped
2 × 14oz (397g) cans of
    tomatoes
1 green pepper, seeded and diced
3 tablespoons tomato purée
3 teaspoons caster sugar
2 teaspoons chilli seasoning
1½lb (675g) cooked chicken, cut
    into bite-sized pieces
salt
freshly ground black pepper
¾ pint (450 ml) soured cream
12 tortillas
12oz (350g) well flavoured
    Cheddar cheese, grated

Not all Mexican dishes are hot and spicy. This is a bit like a lasagne, and is delicious served hot with crusty bread and a mixed green salad. Tortillas are available in many delicatessens, continental grocers and good supermarkets.

Start by preparing the chicken sauce. Heat the butter and oil in a large pan and fry the onion for about 10 minutes until soft. Add the contents of the cans of tomatoes, the green pepper, tomato purée, sugar and chilli seasoning. Simmer gently for about 15 minutes until thick and pulpy, then stir in the chicken and seasoning. Remove from the heat.

Heat the oven to 350°F/180°C/Gas Mark 4.

To assemble the pie, spread a third of the chicken sauce in the bottom of a large shallow ovenproof dish, and pour over a third of the cream. Lay six of the tortillas on top of this so they are lying flat and just overlapping. Repeat this with the chicken sauce, cream and tortillas, and then finish with a layer of chicken sauce and cream with the grated cheese sprinkled liberally over the top. Cook in the oven for about 40 minutes until cooked through and the cheese has melted and is golden brown.

Serve hot with lots of crusty bread and salad.

Empanadas

14oz (395g) packet of frozen
    puff pastry, thawed
1 quantity cold Picadillo
    (page 120)
a little beaten egg

These savoury turnovers are good to serve on a buffet table as they can easily be picked up and eaten in the fingers.

Heat the oven to 425°F/220°C/Gas Mark 7.

Roll out the pastry on a lightly floured surface and cut out twelve 6 inch (15cm) circles: I use a saucer to measure these. Spoon 2 good tablespoons of the Picadillo into the middle of each of the circles. Brush the outside edge of the circle with beaten egg and fold over and seal the edges together. Arrange the Empanadas on a baking tray and brush with beaten egg. Mark two small slits in the top with a knife and bake in the oven for about 20 minutes until well risen and golden brown and the pastry underneath is cooked. These can be made ahead and then reheated as required (in a hot oven for about 15 minutes).

Vegetarian Chilli

It is always useful to have one or two vegetarian recipes at hand. This mixture of vegetables has a wonderful flavour and will be enjoyed by meat eaters too. Serve with rice or crusty French bread and butter.

Heat the oven to 350°F/180°C/Gas Mark 4.

Heat the butter and oil in a large fireproof casserole pan and fry the onions and garlic for about 10 minutes until soft and beginning to brown. Add the pepper, courgettes and celery and fry quickly for another 2 minutes, then stir in all the remaining ingredients. Bring to the boil, cover with a lid and cook in the oven for about an hour until the vegetables are tender. Taste and check seasoning and serve hot with rice or French bread.

2oz (50g) butter
1 tablespoon sunflower oil
2 large onions, chopped
2 fat cloves of garlic, crushed
1 large green pepper, seeded and diced
1lb (450g) courgettes, sliced
4 sticks of celery, chopped
8oz (225g) button mushrooms, sliced
1 large aubergine, sliced and blanched in boiling salted water for a minute
1 tablespoon chilli seasoning
salt
freshly ground black pepper
2 tablespoons caster sugar
2 × 14oz (397g) cans of tomatoes
2 tablespoons tomato purée
15½oz (439g) can of red kidney beans, drained

Tacos

Tacos are the Mexican equivalent of our 'sandwich'. They are ideal to serve for a buffet as they can easily be eaten in one hand. Do provide napkins, though, if you are generous with the fillings.

Heat the oven to 350°F/180°C/Gas Mark 4. Arrange the tacos shells on a baking tray and heat in the oven for about 10 minutes so they are warmed through. Heat the Picadillo in a large pan until heated through. Arrange a little lettuce in the bottom of each tacos shell, top with a generous helping of Picadillo, then sprinkle with cheese. Serve straightaway.

Serves 12 as part of a buffet

12 tacos shells
1 iceberg lettuce, shredded
1 quantity Picadillo (page 120)
6oz (175g) mature Cheddar cheese, grated

Picadillo

2lb (900g) minced beef
1 large onion, chopped
2 fat cloves of garlic, crushed
1 green pepper, seeded and
  chopped
¾ pint (450 ml) good beef stock
2 boiled potatoes, roughly diced
2oz (50g) blanched almonds,
  roughly chopped
2oz (50g) raisins
4 good tablespoons tomato purée
1 tablespoon chilli seasoning
1 tablespoon caster sugar
salt
freshly ground black pepper

This is the Mexican version of our savoury mince. It can either be served hot with rice or used as a filling for Tacos shells or Empanadas.

Heat the minced beef gently in a non-stick pan until the fat begins to run out, then increase the heat and add the onion and garlic. Fry for about 10 minutes until the onion has softened and the meat has browned. Stir in the remaining ingredients and bring to the boil, cover with a lid and simmer gently for about 25 minutes until the meat is tender, stirring from time to time.

Serve hot with plenty of rice and perhaps a crisp green salad.

Refried Beans

2 tablespoons sunflower oil
1 small onion, chopped
8oz (225g) dried red kidney
  beans, soaked overnight and
  cooked in boiling salted water
  until really soft
2 teaspoons chilli seasoning

I don't think these are particularly good on their own but they make an excellent base for Tostadas, dips and soups.

Heat the oil in a large pan, add the onion and fry for about 5 minutes until softened. Add the beans and chilli seasoning and cook gently, mashing the beans down with a potato masher whilst they cook. Once mashed down, cook until a thick porridge consistency, stirring to prevent the mixture sticking. Use as suggested above, or serve as an accompaniment to a Mexican dish topped with a little finely chopped onion.

Makes about ½ pint (300 ml)

Mango Icecream

A rather unusual icecream, with a wonderful fruit flavour.

Peel the mangos and remove the stones. Process the flesh in a processor or blender to a smooth purée. Whisk the egg yolks in a bowl until blended. In a large bowl whisk the egg whites with an electric whisk until stiff, then whisk in the sugar a teaspoon at a time. Whisk the cream in a separate bowl until it forms soft peaks and fold it into the egg whites with the mango purée and yolks until evenly blended (I find it easiest to use a wire whisk for this). Turn the mixture into a large clean plastic container, cover with a lid, label and freeze until required.

To serve, leave at room temperature for about 5 minutes then scoop into tall stemmed glasses and serve with crisp thin biscuits or brandy snaps.

Serves up to 16

2 ripe mangos
8 eggs, separated
8oz (225g) caster sugar
1 pint (600 ml) double cream

DANISH BUFFET

For a lunch buffet the Danes would more than likely lay out a huge spread of bread, cheeses, pickled fish, cold meats and salads for guests to help themselves – the famous open table or Smörgåsbord. Denmark is also renowned for its wonderful open sandwiches – Smørrebrød – but they also prepare mini versions of these which are known as Snitter (page 125). These are ideal to serve at a drinks party on a Sunday evening, say, as most people will have enjoyed a traditional Sunday lunch earlier, and they are easy to pick up and eat in the fingers.

The Smörgåsbord can contain hot dishes too, like the Frikadeller (page 127). Start a buffet supper off with a touch of luxury, giving everyone a small open sandwich of smoked salmon on a plate decorated with a sprig of fresh dill and a wedge of lemon. Serve a mustard sauce separately (page 128). For twenty-four people buy 1½lb (675g) sliced smoked salmon. If the budget doesn't run to this, make a small open sandwich – a Snitter – with a Herring and Mayonnaise topping (page 125) instead.

Serve the meat with schnapps or aquavit. Beer or lager chasers are traditional too!

Menu

SUNDAY NIGHT SNITTER SUPPER FOR 12

Watercress Soup
(page 33)

Selection of Snitter

Rödgröd

Preparation Hints

Watercress Soup

Make ahead and reheat, but do not boil or it will lose its colour. You could stir in some single cream.

Snitter

Can be prepared an hour or so ahead and arranged in the kitchen for people to help themselves. Arrange them on a big tray or wooden board. I allow about three snitter each, depending on size. If they are on the large side, you will need a knife and fork; if small they can be eaten with the fingers.

Rödgröd

Can be made ahead and chilled.

Menu

DANISH BUFFET PARTY FOR 24

Smoked Salmon with Sweet Mustard Sauce

2 × Danish Frikadeller with Good Onion Sauce

2 × Spiced Red Cabbage

2 × Cucumber and Dill Salad

2 × Danish Caramelised Potatoes

Peasant Girl with Veil

Apricot and Almond Flan
(page 65)

Cheeseboard

Preparation Hints

Smoked Salmon with Sweet Mustard Sauce

Slice the salmon in advance and cover with clingfilm. Make the sauce in advance.

Danish Frikadeller

Can be made and fried ahead of time. Keep them hot.

Onion Sauce

Make but do not mix with the meatballs otherwise they will lose their crispness.

Spiced Red Cabbage

Can be made the day before and reheated.

Cucumber and Dill Salad

Make on the day.

Danish Caramelised Potatoes

These can be kept warm for a reasonable amount of time.

Peasant Girl with Veil

Can be made well in advance.

The breadcrumbs can be made days ahead and kept in the freezer.

Apricot and Almond Flan

Reheats well.

Cheeseboard

This should major on Danish Blue, of course, but there are lots of other interesting Danish cheeses stocked in most good cheese shops and cheese departments.

Smoked Mackerel Bites

Tiny rounds of fried bread topped with a little smoked mackerel pâté, one bite big!

With a small pastry cutter, cut the bread into small rounds about 1 inch (2.5cm) in diameter. Heat the oil in a pan and fry a few of the rounds at a time until crisp and golden brown. Drain thoroughly on kitchen paper.

For the pâté, skin and bone the smoked mackerel and put into a processor or blender with the butter, cream cheese, lemon juice and pepper. Process until smooth. Taste to check seasoning. Turn into a bowl, cover and keep cool until required.

To assemble, spoon the pâté into a piping bag fitted with a star-shaped nozzle and pipe a swirl of pâté on to each round of bread. Garnish with a small sprig of parsley in the middle.

Will make about 30, depending on the size of the cutter

5 slices of white bread
a little oil, for frying

For the pâté
8oz (225g) smoked mackerel
8oz (225g) butter, melted
4oz (100g) rich cream cheese
juice of ½ lemon
freshly ground black pepper
parsley for garnish

Snitter

These are small Danish open sandwiches to eat in the fingers. Choose from the toppings listed below and offer a selection served on small pieces of pumpernickel, rye or brown bread. Slice the bread thinly and divide each slice into four small squares. Spread thinly with butter and arrange the various toppings on top.

Herring and Mayonnaise

Drain the liquid from an 8oz (250g) jar of Marina herring fillets (salt herrings in a sweet wine sauce). Slice the fillets into thin strips and put in a bowl with 2 tablespoons lemon juice, 3 tablespoons mayonnaise (page 41) and ¼ teaspoon ground turmeric. Mix well. Arrange a layer of shredded lettuce on top of buttered granary bread and top with a little of the herring mixture.

Makes 6

Sliced Egg and Curried Mayonnaise

Arrange slices of hard-boiled eggs on top of 6 pieces of bread, spread with a little curried mayonnaise (page 41) and decorate with a pinch of paprika pepper.

Makes 6

Prawns in Dill Mayonnaise

Toss 8oz (225g) peeled prawns in 4 tablespoons dill mayonnaise (page 41). Spoon on top of the pieces of pumpernickel or rye bread and decorate with a small sprig of dill.

Makes 6

Danish Blue and Grape

Arrange thin slivers of Danish Blue cheese on slices of bread and decorate with half a black grape, seeded, with the cut side down.

Scrambled Egg

Spoon scrambled egg on top of the buttered bread, and decorate with a little black lumpfish roe.

Smoked Salmon Pâté

Spread a little smoked salmon pâté (page 55) on the bread, and decorate with a little red lumpfish roe or small sprigs of parsley.

Danish Gammon with Peaches

It is always advisable to soak a piece of gammon overnight before cooking as it can be salty, but do ask your butcher first.

Place the gammon in a pan just large enough to hold it, along with the bay leaves, peppercorns and onion, and pour over enough cider just to cover the joint. Bring to the boil, cover with a lid and simmer very gently for 20 minutes per lb (450g) plus an extra 20 minutes. When cooked, lift out and leave until cool enough to handle. Carefully peel off the skin and mark the fat into diamond shapes with a sharp knife.

Heat the oven to 400°F/200°C/Gas Mark 6.

For the glaze, measure the mustard, soy sauce, sugar and ginger into a small bowl. Drain the peaches, reserving the syrup, and put them in an ovenproof dish. Add 6 tablespoons of the peach syrup to the glaze and mix well. Pour the remainder back over the peaches and put in the oven to heat through whilst the oven is warming up.

Put the gammon in an ovenproof serving dish, spoon over the glaze and cook in the oven for about 10 minutes until the glaze is shiny and bubbling. Remove from the oven and serve the gammon cut in slices with a little of the glaze, a peach, and a little of the juice with each slice.

4lb (1.8kg) piece of Danish corner gammon, boned and rolled
3 bay leaves
peppercorns
1 onion, sliced
cider
4 teaspoons dry mustard
2 tablespoons soy sauce
4 tablespoons light muscovado sugar
1 level teaspoon ground ginger
2 × 15oz (425g) cans of peach halves

Danish Frikadeller

Be sure to chill the mixture well between processes as this makes it easier to handle and helps the frikadeller to keep their shape during cooking.

Heat the butter and 1 tablespoon oil in a pan and fry the onion for about 10 minutes until golden brown. Turn into a bowl, add the remaining ingredients, seasoning well. Mix well until thoroughly blended: I tend to use my hands for this. Cover with clingfilm and chill in the refrigerator for several hours until really cold.

To shape the frikadeller, take good dessertspoonfuls of the mixture and with lightly floured hands shape into oval, egg shapes. Return to the refrigerator for about 2 hours before cooking.

To cook, heat the remaining oil in a large pan and gently fry the frikadeller for about 15 minutes until golden brown all over. Serve hot with Good Onion Sauce and Spiced Red Cabbage.

2oz (50g) butter
4 tablespoons sunflower oil
2 large onions, chopped
1lb (450g) minced pork
2lb (900g) minced beef
6oz (175g) fresh brown breadcrumbs
4fl. oz (120 ml) milk
3 eggs, beaten
salt
freshly ground black pepper

Good Onion Sauce

3oz (75g) butter
1lb (450g) onions, sliced
3oz (75g) flour
2 pints (1.2 litres) good stock
6 tablespoons tomato ketchup
1 teaspoon Worcestershire sauce
½ teaspoon dried marjoram
salt
freshly ground black pepper

This sauce goes particularly well with Frikadeller but I also like to serve it with the Picnic Loaves (page 34).

Heat the butter in a pan and fry the onion for about 10 minutes until golden brown. Stir in the flour and cook for a minute, then gradually blend in the stock. Bring to the boil, stirring until the sauce has thickened. Add the ketchup, Worcestershire sauce, majoram, salt and pepper, and stir well. Cover with a lid and simmer gently for about 20 minutes.

Sweet Mustard Sauce

8oz (225g) soft brown sugar
4 level tablespoons dried mustard
    powder
6 tablespoons sunflower oil
6 tablespoons water
salt
freshly ground black pepper
2 teaspoons dried dill weed

Delicious to serve with smoked or fresh salmon.

Measure the sugar and the mustard into a pan and gradually blend in the oil and the water until smooth. Heat gently, stirring all the time until the sugar has dissolved and the sauce has thickened slightly. Remove from the heat and add seasoning to taste and the dill weed.

Allow to cool, then turn into a serving bowl and serve well chilled with cold fish such as smoked salmon, fresh salmon or trout.

Danish Caramelised Potatoes

5lb (2.25kg) baby new potatoes,
    scraped
4oz (100g) sugar
4oz (100g) butter
freshly chopped parsley, to serve

If possible, choose tiny new potatoes for this recipe: they are now available most of the year round in good supermarkets. After caramelising, they are very sweet, and if you might not like this, prepare plain boiled potatoes – which is again very Danish.

Cook the potatoes in a large pan of boiling salted water for about 10 minutes. Rinse under running cold water then drain thoroughly. Wipe out the pan and heat the sugar until it is light brown, then add the butter. Toss the potatoes in the caramel until they are golden brown. It is essential either to use a very large pan for this or to cook the potatoes in two batches so that they can be browned without breaking up.

Turn the potatoes into a warm serving dish, cover with foil and keep warm in a moderate oven until required. Serve sprinkled with freshly chopped parsley.

Spiced Red Cabbage

Red cabbage is served a great deal in Denmak with Frikadeller. I also serve it with grilled meats such as pork or lamb chops.

Put the cabbage, apples, water, sugar, salt and cloves into a large pan. Bring to the boil, cover with a lid and simmer gently for about 45 minutes or until tender. Remove and discard the cloves, and stir in the vinegar, butter and redcurrant jelly. Cook over a gentle heat, stirring continuously until the butter has melted. Taste and adjust seasoning then turn into a warmed serving dish.

1 large red cabbage, shredded
1½lb (675g) cooking apples, peeled, cored and sliced
scant ½ pint (300 ml) water
2oz (50g) demerara sugar
salt
6 cloves
¼ pint (150 ml) white wine vinegar
4oz (100g) butter
3 tablespoons redcurrant jelly

Cucumber and Dill Salad

This salad goes particularly well with fish dishes such as trout, but I like to include it on most buffet tables since it is so light and refreshing.

Peel the cucumbers, and cut in half lengthwise. Scoop out the seeds then cut the flesh thinly to give 'moon' shapes of cucumbers. Arrange these in a serving dish.

Blend the oil, water, vinegar, sugar and seasoning together and pour over the cucumber. Cover with clingfilm and chill in the refrigerator for several hours before serving sprinkled with chopped dill.

2 cucumbers
2 tablespoons sunflower oil
4 tablespoons hot water
4 tablespoons white wine vinegar
4 tablespoons caster sugar
salt
freshly ground black pepper
a little freshly chopped dill

Serves 12 with other salads

Rödgröd

3lb (1.4kg) mixed soft fruits
(redcurrants, raspberries,
blackcurrants and
strawberries)
2 pints (1.2 litres) water
1lb (450g) granulated sugar
about 3–4 tablespoons arrowroot
a little extra sugar, to sprinkle on
top

This dish is a fruit custard which is just lightly set.

Measure the fruits and water into a pan and bring to the boil. Cover with a lid and simmer gently for about 5 minutes or until tender. Remove from the heat and stir in the sugar. Reduce the fruity liquid to a purée in a processor or blender, then sieve to remove all the seeds (it may be necessary to do this in batches).

Measure the quantity of fruit syrup and for each pint (600 ml) blend 1 level tablespoon arrowroot in a little cold water. Stir arrowroot into the fruit syrup and return to the pan. Bring to the boil, stirring until thickened. Allow to cool slightly then divide between twelve individual serving glasses. Sprinkle the tops with a little sugar to prevent a skin from forming, and chill well in the refrigerator before serving.

Peasant Girl with Veil

4lb (1.75kg) cooking apples,
peeled, cored and sliced
juice of 2 lemons
about 8oz (225g) caster sugar
4oz (100g) butter
1lb (450g) fresh brown (or rye)
breadcrumbs
6oz (175g) light muscovado
sugar

To decorate
½ pint (300 ml) whipping
cream, whipped
a little plain chocolate, grated

This is a really quick and simple dessert to prepare for a party. It can be prepared well in advance, kept in the refrigerator then decorated just before serving.

Measure the apples into a pan with the lemon juice, cover with a lid and cook gently for about 10 minutes until the apples are tender. Remove from the heat, stir in the caster sugar to taste, and leave to cool.

Heat the butter in a large pan and quickly fry the breadcrumbs for about 5 minutes until golden brown. Remove from the heat, allow to cool slightly and stir in the sugar.

To assemble the dessert, have ready twelve individual glasses. Spoon the apple and breadcrumb mixture in alternate layers into the glasses, starting with a layer of apple and finishing with a layer of the breadcrumbs. Chill in the refrigerator until required and serve with a swirl of cream piped on top and sprinkled with grated chocolate.

ITALIAN BUFFET

Italian pasta recipes are especially suitable for a buffet party as they are warm, welcoming and most keep hot well. The table could represent the Italian colours of red, green and yellow, and it could be fun to have the party in the garden if the weather is fine.

I think my favourite dish in this section is the Mozzarella and Spinach Lasagne. This, however, should not be kept warm in the oven for too long otherwise the spinach will lose its wonderful, bright green colour. The Risotto with Chicken Liver Sauce has rather a different flavour from the usual risotto, and is good to serve in small portions as a first course; it can be turned out on to serving plates and kept warm, and then the sauce poured over the top just before serving. Spaghetti Carbonara is ideal for a small buffet party of about twelve guests, and should be served as soon as it is cooked. Unless you have some help, I wouldn't attempt to make any larger quantity all in one go.

Whenever I have served an Italian buffet meal, I usually offer an ice-cream for the pudding, for the Italians are as famous for their icecream as they are for their pasta. Try the Gelato Amaretti Icecream or the Zabaglione, both of which are very Italian.

Drink Italian wine with the meals, obviously! Chianti is perhaps the most well known, and it is delicious with pasta and red meats. Campari as a drink before the meal would be traditional: add orange slices, ice cubes and soda and mix well.

Menu

LATE NIGHT SUPPER PARTY FOR 12

Antipasti

Tuna Noodle Bake

Stuffed Green Peppers

French bread

Italian Tomato Salad

Gelato Amaretti Icecream

Preparation Hints

Antipasti

Could be prepared on big trays in advance, covered in clingfilm and put into a cool place until needed. Make double of each, leaving out the Tuna Salad.

Tuna Noodle Bake

Prepare in advance and put it into the oven as soon as you come in.

Stuffed Green Peppers

Prepare and half cook them before going out. Complete cooking on your return.

Italian Tomato Salad

Can be prepared before you go out.

Menu

ITALIAN KITCHEN BUFFET FOR 12

Tuna and Tomato Salad

Italian Chicken

Mozzarella and Spinach Lasagne

French beans

Cheese Bread Rolls

Zabaglione

Preparation Hints

Tuna and Tomato Salad
Can be made in advance as it needs to be chilled well before serving.

Italian Chicken
Can be cooked, cooled and frozen. Reheat and scatter with parsley.

Mozzarella and Spinach Lasagne
Can be prepared ahead.

French beans
For twelve people, you will need 3lb (1.4kg) French beans. Use fresh if in season, or frozen. Cook them until they are still a little crunchy and top with butter and black pepper.

Cheese Bread Rolls
Can be baked well in advance.

Zabaglione
Have all the ingredients ready, then tip them into a bowl and whisk.

Antipasti

This is a colourful salad dish which may be served as an hors d'oeuvres. Serve either on individual plates or on one large platter, arranging the salads and cold meat in sections around the plate so they give a cartwheel effect.

Eggs in Mayonnaise

Halve 6 hard-boiled eggs lengthwise and lay cut-side down along the edges of the serving plate. Spoon a little mayonnaise (page 41) over each of the eggs and decorate with a criss-cross of halved anchovy fillets.

Tomato and Onion

Slice 1lb (450g) tomatoes and mix with a small finely sliced onion. Lightly toss in a little French dressing and spoon on to the serving plate alongside the egg. Sprinkle with a few freshly chopped chives.

Salami Rolls

Roll up slices of salami, allowing three rolls per person and arrange next to the tomato.

Fennel Salad

Finely slice a small head of fennel, and mix with 4 chopped sticks of celery. Toss in a little French dressing and arrange on the plate on a bed of watercress next to the salami.

Tuna Salad

Roughly mix the contents of four 7oz (200g) cans of tuna fish with the contents of a 15oz (425g) can of haricot beans and a little French dressing. Take care not to mash the fish, it just needs roughly flaking. Arrange on the plate next to the fennel and decorate with a little finely sliced onion.

Iceberg Salad

Finely shred a small iceberg lettuce and toss in a little French dressing with a teaspoon of dried dill weed. Arrange on the plate between the tuna and the eggs.

Tuna and Tomato Salad

These tiny tomatoes are firm and easy to skin. A very colourful salad which makes a good first course.

Mix the onions and dressing together in a bowl and leave to stand whilst preparing the other ingredients. Blanch the beans in a pan of boiling salted water for 3 minutes, refresh under running cold water and drain thoroughly. Skin the tomatoes: mark a small cross in the stalk end of the tomatoes with a sharp knife and place in a bowl, and cover with boiling water. Leave for a few moments until the skins of the tomatoes are beginning to come away then rinse under cold water, when the skins will slip off easily.

Toss the beans, tomatoes and tuna in the spring onion dressing and season well with salt and pepper. Turn into a serving dish and chill well before serving.

12 spring onions, finely sliced
9 tablespoons French dressing
  (page 42)
1½lb (675g) French beans,
  topped and tailed
1½lb (675g) cherry tomatoes
3 × 7oz (198g) cans of tuna fish,
  drained and roughly flaked
salt
freshly ground black pepper

Tuna Noodle Bake

This tuna sauce can be served with any variety of pasta. In our family tagliatelle is a firm favourite but the recipe works well with spaghetti, macaroni and pasta shells.

Cook the tagliatelle in a large pan of boiling salted water as directed on the packet until just tender. Drain and rinse well under running hot water. Heat the oven to 350°F/180°C/Gas Mark 4.

For the sauce, melt the butter in a pan, add the mushrooms and gently fry for about 3 minutes until soft. Stir in the flour and cook for a minute then gradually blend in the milk and bring to the boil, stirring until thickened. Remove from the heat and stir in the seasoning, tuna fish and eggs. Pour the sauce over the tagliatelle and toss lightly until the pasta is evenly coated in sauce. Taste and check seasoning.

Transfer to a large ovenproof serving dish, sprinkle with cheese and bake in the oven for about 50 minutes until the sauce is bubbling and the cheese has melted and is golden brown. Sprinkle with chopped parsley and serve hot with a tomato or tossed green salad.

1lb (450g) tagliatelle
3oz (75g) butter
8oz (225g) button mushrooms,
  sliced
3oz (75g) flour
2 pints (1.2 litres) milk
salt
freshly ground black pepper
4 × 7oz (198g) cans of tuna fish,
  drained
8 hard-boiled eggs, shelled and
  quartered
8oz (225g) well flavoured
  Cheddar cheese, grated
a little freshly chopped parsley,
  to serve

Risotto with Chicken Liver Sauce

2oz (50g) butter
2 tablespoons sunflower oil
2 medium onions, chopped
1lb (450g) long-grain rice
about 1½ pints (900 ml) good
    chicken stock
salt
freshly ground black pepper

For the meat sauce
2oz (50g) butter
2 tablespoons sunflower oil
2 medium onions, chopped
2 fat cloves of garlic, crushed
4oz (100g) streaky bacon,
    chopped
8oz (225g) minced beef
1lb (450g) chicken livers,
    roughly chopped
1 teaspoon dried sage
salt
freshly ground black pepper
2 tablespoons tomato purée
¼ pint (150 ml) dry white
    vermouth
¼ pint (150 ml) good chicken
    stock
sprigs of watercress and wedges of
    tomato, to garnish

Garnish small mounds of risotto with sprigs of watercress and wedges of tomato, and serve as a first course. Larger portions could be served as a main course. The risottos and sauce can be prepared ahead and kept warm for a short while then, to serve, spoon a little of the sauce on top of each risotto.

For the risotto, heat the butter and the oil in a large pan and fry the onion for about 5 minutes until beginning to soften. Stir in the rice and cook for a minute then add about three-quarters of the stock. Cover with a lid and simmer gently for about 15 minutes, stirring occasionally, until the rice is just tender and all the liquid has been absorbed. Add a little more stock as necessary during cooking so that the rice when cooked is moist but not wet. Remove from the heat and season to taste with salt and pepper. Lightly butter a small ramekin dish and fill with risotto, pressing down firmly. Turn out on to a warm serving plate. Repeat with the remaining mixture and keep warm in the oven.

For the meat sauce, heat the butter and the oil in a large pan and fry the onion and the garlic for about 5 minutes until beginning to soften. Stir in the bacon, minced beef and chicken livers and cook for about 5 minutes until they have browned. Stir in the remaining ingredients and simmer gently for about 15 minutes until the meats are tender. Taste and check seasoning.

To serve, spoon a little of the meat sauce on top of each of the mounds of risotto. Garnish with watercress and tomato.

Serves 12 as a first course

Mozzarella and Spinach Lasagne

This dish cannot be kept warm in the oven for long as the spinach will begin to lose its lovely bright colour, and the cheese will become tough. It can, however, be prepared well ahead and then kept in the refrigerator until required and cooked as suggested in the recipe. Serve with crisp French bread.

For the meat sauce, measure the minced beef, pork and chopped bacon into a large non-stick pan and heat gently until the fat begins to run out, then increase the heat and fry quickly until browned. Add the onions and celery and cook for 5 minutes. Sprinkle in the flour followed by all the remaining ingredients for the meat sauce, stir well and bring to the boil. Cover with a lid and simmer gently, stirring from time to time for about an hour until the meat is tender.

For the white sauce, melt the butter in a large pan, stir in the flour and cook for a minute. Gradually blend in the milk and bring to the boil, stirring until thickened. Remove from the heat and stir in the nutmeg, salt, pepper and mustard. Taste and check seasoning of both sauces.

In a large shallow ovenproof dish put a third of the meat sauce, a third of the white sauce and a third of the cheese slices, followed by half the uncooked lasagne (be sure not to overlap the sheets). Spread half the spinach over this then start again with a third of meat sauce, white sauce and cheese and the last half of the lasagne and the spinach. Repeat, finishing with a final layer of meat sauce, white sauce and sliced cheese with the grated cheeses on top. Leave to become cold.

To serve, heat the oven to 350°F/180°C/Gas Mark 4, and cook the lasagne for about 1–1¼ hours until the top is golden brown and the sauce is bubbling.

10oz (275g) uncooked Barilla lasagne
2 × 10.6oz (about 300g) packets frozen cut-leaf spinach, thawed and thoroughly drained
12oz (350g) Mozzarella cheese, thinly sliced
4oz (100g) well flavoured Cheddar cheese, grated
1oz (25g) Parmesan cheese, grated

For the meat sauce
1lb (450g) minced beef
1lb (450g) minced pork
2oz (50g) streaky bacon, chopped
2 large onions, chopped
6 sticks of celery, chopped
1oz (25g) flour
1 pint (600 ml) good stock
6 tablespoons tomato purée
4 fat cloves of garlic, crushed
3 teaspoons sugar
salt
freshly ground black pepper
½ teaspoon mixed dried herbs

For the white sauce
2oz (50g) butter
2oz (50g) flour
1½ pints (900 ml) milk
ground nutmeg
salt
freshly ground black pepper
2 teaspoons Dijon mustard

Tomato Baked Noodles

1oz (25g) butter
1 tablespoon sunflower oil
2 large onions, chopped
2 × 15oz (425g) cans of
  tomatoes
6 tablespoons tomato purée
2 teaspoons sugar
salt
freshly ground black pepper
1lb (450g) ribbon noodles
1lb (450g) well flavoured
  Cheddar cheese, thinly sliced
3oz (75g) Parmesan cheese,
  grated

Serve instead of a potato dish with barbecued chicken drumsticks and cold meat with salads. For convenience, you can prepare it all well ahead and then just reheat as below.

Start by preparing the sauce. Heat the butter and oil in a large pan and quickly fry the onion until soft and beginning to brown. Stir in the contents of the cans of tomatoes, the purée, sugar, salt and pepper. Bring to the boil and simmer gently for about 15 minutes until thick and pulpy. Taste and check seasoning.

Cook the ribbon noodles as directed on the packet in a pan of boiling salted water until just tender. Drain and rinse under running hot water.

To assemble the dish, arrange the noodles, tomato sauce and cheeses in layers in a lightly buttered large ovenproof dish, finishing with a layer of cheese on top. To serve, cook in the oven at 375°F/190°C/Gas Mark 5 for about 45 minutes until the sauce is bubbling and the cheese is golden brown.

Spaghetti Carbonara

12oz (350g) streaky bacon,
  chopped
2 fat cloves of garlic, crushed
2lb (900g) spaghetti
12 eggs
8oz (225g) Parmesan cheese,
  grated
salt
freshly ground black pepper
½ pint (300 ml) single cream

This is the sort of supper buffet dish that can be served after a trip to the cinema or theatre. All the ingredients can be prepared ahead, the garlic and bacon fried the tagliatelle weighed out and the eggs beaten with the cheese then the dish just needs assembling when you come back in. Really quick and easy to prepare and delicious served with a crisp green salad.

Cook the bacon in a non-stick pan over a gentle heat until the fat begins to run out, then increase the heat. Add the garlic and fry quickly until the bacon is crisp. Meanwhile, cook the spaghetti in a large pan of boiling salted water as directed on the packet. Break the eggs into a bowl, add the cheese and plenty of seasoning, and beat well until blended.

When the spaghetti is cooked, drain thoroughly and return to the hot pan. Add the bacon and the egg mixture, and cook over a moderate heat, stirring continuously, until the egg is lightly set. Stir in the cream and continue to cook until heated through then serve straight away with salad.

Italian Chicken

Serve two chicken thighs per person. If the buffet is to be eaten with a fork then either buy boned chicked thighs or bone the thighs before cooking.

Heat the oven to 350°F/180°C/Gas Mark 4.

Heat the butter and oil in a large pan and quickly fry the chicken thighs until browned all over. Lift out with a slotted spoon and arrange in a large ovenproof casserole dish. It may be necessary to fry the chicken in batches.

Add the onion, carrot and celery to the fat remaining in the pan and fry for about 10 minutes until the onion has softened and is beginning to brown. Stir in the contents of the cans of tomatoes, the purée and the stock. Bring to the boil and allow to simmer until the sauce has reduced to a fairly thick consistency. Add half the parsley, the marjoram, sugar, salt and pepper then spoon over the chicken thighs. Cover with a lid and bake in the oven for about 1¼ hours until the chicken is tender. Taste and check seasoning then serve piping hot, sprinkled with freshly chopped parsley, and with puréed potato to sop up the sauce.

2oz (50g) butter
2 tablespoons sunflower oil
24 chicken thighs
2 large onions, chopped
4 large carrots, sliced
6 sticks of celery, chopped
2 × 15oz (425g) cans of tomatoes
4oz (100g) can of tomato purée
½ pint (300 ml) good chicken stock
4 tablespoons freshly chopped parsley
2 teaspoons dried marjoram
2 teaspoons sugar
salt
freshly ground black pepper

Italian Tomato Salad

If fresh basil is not available, then use a few snipped chives or spring onion tops, roughly chopped.

Slice the tomatoes and arrange on a large serving platter so that they overlap. Arrange the rings of onion on top of this. Stir the chopped basil into the French dressing and spoon over the salad. Season with salt and pepper, and chill until required.

Serves 12 with a choice of other salads

8 beefsteak tomatoes
1 small onion, thinly sliced into rings
about 10 leaves of fresh basil, chopped
6 tablespoons French dressing (page 42)
salt
freshly ground black pepper

Stuffed Aubergines

6 aubergines
2lb (900g) raw lean lamb,
   minced
2 large onions, chopped
2 fat cloves of garlic, crushed
2 × 14oz (397g) cans of
   tomatoes
8oz (225g) fresh white
   breadcrumbs
1 teaspoon dried basil
salt
freshly ground black pepper

For the sauce
3 × 8½oz (240g) jars Prego
   Tuscany sauce
¼ pint (150 ml) natural yoghurt

This supper dish is really quite simple to prepare. I like to serve it with plenty of salad and crisp French bread. Blanching the aubergine removes the bitter juices from the vegetable and ensures that it will be cooked throughout when it comes out of the oven.

Heat the oven to 350°F/180°C/Gas Mark 4.

Cut the aubergines in half lengthwise and blanch in a pan of boiling water for 2 minutes then refresh in cold water. It is easiest to do this in batches. Scoop the middles out of the aubergines and keep on one side. Arrange the aubergine skins in the bottom of a shallow ovenproof dish so they are just touching.

Gently cook the lamb in a non-stick pan until the fat begins to run freely from the meat then increase the heat and fry until browned. Add the onion and garlic and cook for a few more minutes until beginning to soften. Stir in the contents of the cans of tomatoes, three-quarters of the breadcrumbs, the middle from the aubergines, the basil and plenty of seasoning. Mix well. Divide the meat mixture between the aubergine skins. Sprinkle with the remaining breadcrumbs and bake in the oven for about 45 minutes until the aubergines are tender and the breadcrumbs are a golden brown.

For the sauce, empty the contents of the jars of Tuscany sauce into a pan and bring to the boil. Stir in the yoghurt and reheat, but do not allow to boil. To serve, pour a little of the sauce over each aubergine half.

Stuffed Green Peppers

A good buffet supper dish to serve in the summer when peppers are at their cheapest. I like to accompany it with warm crisp French bread.

Cut a circle from the base of each of the peppers to remove the stem and seeds. Arrange the peppers in a shallow ovenproof dish so that they are just touching.

Cook the rice in a pan of boiling salted water as directed on the packet, and do remember that brown rice takes longer to cook than white rice. Drain and rinse well. Melt the butter in a large pan and fry the onion, mushrooms, bacon and chicken livers for about 10 minutes until the onion has softened. Stir in the cooked rice, salt, pepper and parsley. Remove from the heat and stir in the eggs to bind the rice together. Divide this filling between the peppers. Heat the oven to 350°F/180°C/Gas Mark 4.

For the cheese sauce, melt the butter in a large pan, stir in the flour and cook for a minute. Gradually blend in the milk and bring to the boil, stirring until thickened. Remove from the heat and stir in the mustard, a little nutmeg, salt, pepper and about a quarter of the cheese. Mix well and pour the sauce over and around the peppers. Sprinkle with the remaining cheese and bake in the oven for about 1–1¼ hours until the peppers are tender.

12 large even sized green peppers
12 oz (350g) brown long-grain rice
3oz (75g) butter
1 large onion, chopped
12oz (350g) button mushrooms, sliced
8oz back bacon, chopped
8oz (225g) chicken livers, chopped
salt
freshly ground black pepper
3 tablespoons freshly chopped parsley
4 eggs, beaten

For the cheese sauce
4oz (100g) butter
4oz (100g) flour
2 pints (1.2 litres) milk
3 teaspoons made mustard
grated nutmeg
salt
freshly ground black pepper
1lb (450g) well flavoured Cheddar cheese, grated

Garlic Bread

4 fat cloves of garlic
½ teaspoon salt
freshly ground black pepper
8oz (225g) butter, softened
2 French loaves

Delicious with soups and to serve with a buffet, garlic bread can be prepared ahead and frozen until requiired. It then just needs to thaw at room temperature for about 4 hours and then heated though as suggested in the recipe.

Crush the garlic into a bowl and add the salt, pepper and butter. Cream well until thoroughly blended. Cut along the loaf in 1 inch (2.5cm) slices to within ½ inch (1.25cm) of the bottom. Spread the slices on each side with the garlic butter and press together again. Wrap in foil and heat in the oven at 400°F/200°C/Gas Mark 6 for about 15 minutes until hot and crisp, and the butter has melted into the bread.

Serves 12

Cheese Bread Rolls

10oz (283g) packet of white
   bread mix
6oz (175g) well flavoured
   Cheddar cheese, grated
⅓ pint (200 ml) hand-hot water

Quick and simple to prepare and are lovely served with Garlic Mushrooms (page 147) as a first course.

Put the bread mix in a bowl with 5oz (150g) of the cheese, stir in the water, and mix to form a dough. Turn on to a lightly floured surface and knead lightly for 5 minutes until smooth and elastic. Divide into twelve equal pieces and shape into rolls. Place on a lightly greased baking sheet, cover with a piece of greased polythene and leave in a warm place until doubled in bulk (about 30 minutes).

    Whilst the bread is rising heat the oven to 450°F/230°C/Gas Mark 8. Sprinkle the remaining cheese over the rolls and bake in the oven for 10–15 minutes or until well risen and golden brown. Leave to cool on a wire rack.

Makes 12 small bread rolls

Gelato Amaretti Icecream

This icecream is very quick and easy to prepare, and is a great favourite of ours. When preparing it for a party, after processing I pour it into individual serving dishes, such as small ramekins, and then return it to the freezer, which makes serving so much simplier. If you like, just before serving you can decorate each icecream with a blob of whipped cream and an Amaretti biscuit.

1 pint (600 ml) double cream
2 pints (1.2 litres) milk
1½lb (675g) caster sugar
6 teaspoons instant coffee powder dissolved in 1 tablespoon hot water
6 tablespoons whisky
4oz (100g) Amaretti biscuits, roughly crumbled

Measure the cream into a bowl and whisk with an electric whisk until it forms soft peaks, then stir in the milk, sugar, the coffee blended with the hot water, and whisky and mix well until thoroughly blended. Pour into an empty clean icecream container and freeze overnight.

The next day, spoon the icecream into a processor and process until smooth. It will be necessary to do this in batches. Stir the crushed Amaretti biscuits into the processed mixture and either divide into small individual serving dishes that can be frozen, or return to the ice-cream container and freeze until solid.

Allow to thaw at room temperature for about 5 minutes before serving.

Zabaglione

A very simple Italian recipe which is very rich, so serve it after a fairly light meal.

½ pint (300 ml) Madeira, Marsala or sweet sherry
12oz (350g) caster sugar
8 eggs, beaten
4 egg yolks

Stand a large bowl over a pan of simmering water. Measure the Madeira and sugar into the bowl and leave until the mixture is really warm. Add the eggs and yolks and immediately start to whisk with an electric whisk until light and foamy (about 10–15 minutes with an efficient electric whisk).

Divide between twelve tall stemmed serving glasses. Serve straight away with sweet biscuits such as langues de chat or cigarettes russes.

FRENCH BUFFET

A French party is perhaps the most popular cuisine from the Continent. You could even suggest that your guests came dressed appropriately – and expect anything from a can-can girl to a French painter or onion-seller in a black beret! Cover the table with a red check cloth and serve the food in plain earthenware or plain white china, with salads in traditional wooden bowls.

A French occasion might be the 14th July, Bastille Day, and would be lovely in the garden. In colder weather, serve warming stews like Boeuf Bourguignonne or a Mediterranean Fish Casserole. No need for potatoes, as Garlic Bread (page 142) goes well with each. Salads and quiches are delicious for warmer days. Remember, though, always to serve quiches warm, as cold pastry tastes nowhere near as good.

Serve French wines with your French buffets, of course, and you could perhaps start off with Pernod, Pastis, or a Chambéry or vermouth for an authentic *aperitif*. Cognac or one of the host of French liqueurs such as Calvados, would be appropriate after the meal along with the coffee.

Menu

SUMMER LUNCH PARTY FOR 24

2 × Quiche Lorraine

2 × Chicken in Tarragon Cream

Selection of salads

Cheese platter

2 × French Peaches

2 × Caramelised Oranges

Preparation Hints

Quiche Lorraine

Can be made a day ahead but don't contemplate serving unless you serve warm (cold quiche is horrible).

Chicken in Tarragon Cream

Can be made ahead. If you are catering for a larger quantity, as here, you could use a turkey because it is often a much better and more economical buy.

Cheese platter

See hints on page 146.

Puddings

Both can both be made ahead.

Menu

WINTER BUFFET FOR 12

French Onion Soup or Garlic Mushrooms

Sole Florentine

Boeuf Bourguignonne

Boiled new potatoes

Peas and courgettes

French cheeseboard

Chocolate Roulade

Preparation Hints

French Onion Soup

Can be made well ahead. It does pay to have a good stock, whether turkey, chicken or game.

Garlic Mushrooms

Really do need to be made at the last minute, but they are very simple if you have got the ingredients ready.

Sole Florentine

Can be prepared ahead but has to be baked when needed.

Boeuf Bourguignonne

Freezes beautifully.

Peas and Courgettes

Take the same amount of time to cook and their colours will enliven the whole meal. Cook at the last minute and use plenty of black pepper and butter.

French cheeseboard

I like to serve cheese on a board on vine leaves, if you can get them, or blackcurrant leaves, with a bunch of grapes. Don't make too large a choice – just select two or three French cheeses which complement each other and which are in prime condition.

Chocolate Roulade

Can be made in the morning. Cover with clingfilm and chill until needed.

French Onion Soup

A glorious soup to serve when it is cold and the main course is light. Perfect for a family gathering round the fire in winter.

4oz (100g) dripping
3lb (1.4kg) onions, finely chopped
1 level tablespoon sugar
3oz (75g) flour
6 pints (3.5 litres) good beef stock
salt
freshly ground black pepper
12 slices of French bread
6oz (175g) Gruyère cheese, grated

Melt the dripping in a large pan, add the onions and sugar and fry gently, stirring occasionally, until golden brown. Take care not to let them burn otherwise the soup will taste bitter. This will take about 15 minutes.

Stir in the flour and cook for a minute, then gradually blend in the stock, and bring to the boil, stirring until slightly thickened. Add seasoning, cover pan with a lid and simmer for 20 minutes. Taste to check seasoning.

Toast the French bread on one side, then sprinkle the cheese on the untoasted side and put under the grill to melt. Put a slice of bread in each soup bowl and pour the soup over it. Serve at once.

Garlic Mushrooms

Small, fresh, white button mushrooms are best for this dish otherwise the creamy sauce will be grey. Cook just before serving for the best results.

2¼lb (1kg) small button mushrooms
4oz (100g) butter
3 fat cloves of garlic, crushed
salt
freshly ground black pepper
¾ pint (450ml) double cream

Wipe the mushrooms and trim the ends off the stalks. Melt the butter in a large frying pan, add the garlic and mushrooms and cook for about 8 minutes.

Season well, stir in the cream and simmer gently for a further 5 minutes or until the mushrooms are tender. Divide between twelve small dishes and serve hot with Cheese Bread Rolls (page 142).

Quiche Lorraine

8oz (225g) plain flour
2oz (50g) lard
2oz (50g) margarine
about 2 tablespoons water

For the filling
1oz (25g) butter
1 tablespoon sunflower oil
1 large onion, chopped
12oz (350g) streaky bacon,
    snipped into small pieces
8oz (225g) well flavoured
    Cheddar cheese, grated
4 eggs, beaten
½ pint (300 ml) milk
¼ pint (150 ml) single cream
salt
freshly ground black pepper
freshly chopped parsley

Delicious served warm with salad. Can be served as a main dish with salad or as part of a buffet.

Heat the oven to 425°F/220°C/Gas Mark 7, with a thick baking sheet in it.

For the pastry, put the flour in a bowl and rub in the fats until the mixture resembles fine breadcrumbs. Add the water and bind together to form a firm dough. Knead until smooth then roll out on a lightly floured surface and use to line a deep 11 inch (27.5cm) loose-bottomed flan tin. Chill in the refrigerator for about 30 minutes. Line the flan with greaseproof paper and baking beans or a piece of foil and bake in the oven for about 20 minutes; remove the paper and baking beans or foil for the last 5 minutes so the centre of the flan can cook through.

For the filling, heat the butter and oil in a pan and fry the onion and bacon for about 10 minutes until the onion is golden brown and the bacon crisp. Spoon over the base of the flan and sprinkle the cheese on top. In a large jug mix the eggs, milk, cream, seasoning and parsley until thoroughly blended then pour into the flan case. Return the quiche to the oven, reduce the temperature to 350°F/180°C/Gas Mark 4, and cook for about 35 minutes until the filling has set.

Sole Florentine

12 large fillets of sole, skinned
salt
freshly ground black pepper
juice of 2 small lemons
6oz (175g) butter
6oz (175g) flour
3 pints (1.75 litres) milk
3lb (1.4kg) frozen cut-leaf
    spinach, thawed and cooked as
    directed on the packet
6oz (175g) well flavoured
    Cheddar cheese, grated
3oz (75g) fresh white
    breadcrumbs

No need to cook the fish before the dish is assembled.

Heat the oven to 400°F/200°C/Gas Mark 6.

Season the fillets well with salt, pepper and lemon juice and roll up.

Melt the butter in a pan, add the flour and cook for a minute. Gradually blend in the milk and bring to the boil, stirring until thickened. Simmer for 2 minutes and season to taste. Blend 1 pint (600 ml) of the sauce with the spinach and spread in a 6 pint (3.5 litre) ovenproof dish. Arrange the fish on top and pour over the remaining sauce. Mix the cheese and breadcrumbs together and sprinkle on top of the sauce. Bake in the oven for 30–40 minutes until the top is pale brown and the fish perfectly white.

Salmon Roulade

Simply delicious! These pâtés are moulded into a roulade shape in empty con-
densed soup cans with both ends removed. They must be sliced when very
chilled – after 1½ hours in the freezer – and each cut into twelve thin slices.

For the moulds, use two clean empty 10.4oz (295g) condensed soup
cans with both ends removed so they form cylinders. Line the cans
with clingfilm leaving surplus clingfilm at each end. Stretch the slices
of smoked salmon out on two pieces of greaseproof or plain white
paper, each measuring 4 × 8½ inches (10 ×21cm) to cover the whole
of the paper. Carefully roll up and insert into the cans so that the paper
is next to the can and clingfilm.

For the pâté, put the smoked salmon pieces, cream cheese, butter,
lemon juice and pepper into a processor or blender and process until
smooth. Taste to check seasoning. Stand the cylinders on a plate folding the clingfilm over at the bottom to prevent the pâté coming out,
and carefully spoon the pâté into the centre. Fold clingfilm over the
other end and chill very well.

To unmould, carefully take hold of one end of the clingfilm and pull
the pâté out of the tin. Remove clingfilm and paper. Cut each roulade
into twelve slices. Arrange a few leaves of lettuce, endive and raddic-
cio on twelve small plates then top with two slices of pâté. Serve with
wholemeal or granary bread toast and unsalted butter.

8oz (225g) smoked salmon slices
8oz (225g) smoked salmon
*   pieces*
6oz (175g) rich cream cheese
8oz (225g) butter, melted
juice of 1 lemon
freshly ground black pepper

To serve
a few lettuce, endive and radiccio
*   leaves*

Mediterranean Fish Casserole

Serve with plain boiled rice and lots of crisp Garlic Bread (page 142).

Cut the fish into 1 inch (2.5cm) cubes. Melt the butter in a large
shallow pan. Add the onion and fry until almost tender and pale
golden brown. Add the garlic, contents of the cans of tomatoes,
vermouth, thyme and seasoning. Boil rapidly without a lid for 5
minutes to reduce it slightly. Taste to check seasoning. Add the fish
and cook for a further 5 minutes or until the fish is firm and white.
Remove the thyme, turn into a warm serving dish and serve scattered
with freshly chopped parsley and prawns.

3lb (1.4kg) monkfish, skinned
3oz (75g) butter
2 large onions, chopped
2 cloves of garlic, crushed
3 × 14oz (397g) cans tomatoes
¾ pint (450ml) dry vermouth
3 sprigs of lemon thyme
salt and black pepper

To serve
freshly chopped parsley
4oz (100g) peeled prawns,
*   drained*

Boeuf Bourguignonne

3lb (1.4kg) chuck steak
12oz (350g) streaky bacon
1½oz (40g) flour
½ pint (300 ml) good stock
1 pint (600 ml) inexpensive
    Burgundy
2 bay leaves
1 level teaspoon mixed dried
    herbs
salt
freshly ground black pepper
24 small pickling onions
12oz (350g) button mushrooms
freshly chopped parsley, to
    decorate

A real classic French wine casserole, which is particularly good for winter entertaining.

Cut the beef into 1½ inch (3.75cm) cubes, and cut the bacon across into small strips. Put the bacon in a pan and heat gently for 3–4 minutes until the fat begins to run out, then increase the heat and fry the beef with the bacon strips until browned. Lift out with a slotted spoon and put in an ovenproof casserole about 6 pints (3.5 litres) in capacity.

Heat the oven to 325°F/160°C/Gas Mark 3.

Stir the flour into the fat remaining in the pan and cook for a minute. Stir in the stock, wine, bay leaves, herbs and seasoning and bring to the boil, stirring continually. Pour into the casserole. Cover with a lid or piece of foil and cook in the oven for 1½ hours.

Peel the onions, leave them whole and add to the casserole with the mushrooms. Return to the oven for a further hour or until the meat is really tender. Taste to check seasoning. Remove bay leaves. If necessary, skim off any excess fat. Sprinkle with chopped parsley and serve.

Fondue Bourguignonne

Per person
6–8oz (175g–225g) rump steak
sufficient vegetable oil for frying
    (enough to fill each fondue pot
    ⅓ full)

Both the Swiss and the French claim this to be one of their traditional dishes, although cheese fondue is probably the most Swiss. A fondue party is always a fun idea – particularly as the guests end up cooking their own supper! For a party of twelve I find it easiest to borrow fondue stoves from friends so that there can be three or four on the go at the same time.

Cut the meat into cubes ready to fry in the oil. Have ready skewers, each one marked with coloured tape so that each guest will know which is his.

Heat the oil on the hob of the cooker in the kitchen until a faint haze is rising, then transfer it to the fondue stove. Remember that the oil will heat up more quickly with the lid on the pan, but keep an eye on it because it should not become too hot.

Each guest then inserts his skewer with one or two pieces of meat into the oil until the meat is cooked to his taste. The meat should be taken off the skewers, then speared with a dinner fork, which avoids the chance of burning lips.

Keep the oil hot by returning it to the cooker at intervals and try not too cook more than six pieces of meat at a time.

Serve with crisp French bread with butter and a selection of salads, plus a few sauces which may be made in advance.

Curried Mayonnaise

Blend 8 tablespoons mayonnaise (page 41) with juice of ½ lemon, 2 teaspoons curry powder and 2 tablespoons very finely chopped mango chutney.

Mustard and Dill

Blend 8 tablespoons mayonnaise (page 41) with 2 tablespoons Dijon mustard and 1 teaspoon chopped dill.

Chutney

Blend 8 tablespoons mayonnaise (page 41) with chopped chunky tomato chutney or just serve tomato chutney on its own.

Egg and Parsley

Blend 8 tablespoons mayonnaise (page 41) with 2 finely chopped hard-boiled eggs and 2 tablespoons freshly chopped parsley.

You can also serve some additional chutneys and relishes, such as tomato relish, corn relish and wholegrain mustard.

Chicken in Tarragon Cream

2¼lb (1kg) cold cooked chicken,
   cut up into manageable pieces

For the sauce
4 spring onions, chopped
2 teaspoons dried tarragon
2 teaspoons dried chervil
4 tablespoons caster sugar
4 egg yolks
2 teaspoons Dijon mustard
1 × 2oz (50g) can of anchovy
   fillets, drained and cut into
   thin slivers
12 tablespoons sunflower oil
4 tablespoons tarragon or white
   wine vinegar
½ pint (300 ml) whipping
   cream, lightly whipped
salt
freshly ground black pepper

For the garnish
watercress sprigs

This sauce for cold chicken is wonderful. If left in the refrigerator overnight before serving, the flavours will have time to develop and penetrate the chicken.

Put the chopped chicken into a bowl and prepare the sauce. Measure all the ingredients into a bowl and blend together thoroughly. Taste and check seasoning then pour over the chicken and mix well. Turn into a serving dish and leave in the refrigerator overnight to chill. Serve garnished with a few sprigs of watercress.

Serves 10–12

Chocolate Roulade

6 large eggs, separated
5oz (150g) caster sugar
2oz (50g) cocoa
2 tablespoons boiling water

For the filling
icing sugar
½ pint (300 ml) whipping cream
2 tablespoons brandy

A real French classic. Be prepared for it to crack when you roll it up.

Heat the oven to 350°F/180°C/Gas Mark 4. Grease and line a 12 × 8 inch (30 × 20cm) Swiss roll tin with greaseproof paper.
   Put the egg whites in a large bowl and the yolks into a small bowl. Add caster sugar, cocoa and boiling water to the yolks and whisk until thick and creamy. Whisk egg whites until stiff but not dry. Add 2 tablespoons of whisked egg whites to the yolk mixture and mix together. Add yolk mixture to the whites and fold in with a metal spoon until the mixture is an even colour. Pour the roulade mixture gently into the prepared tin. Bake in the oven for about 20 minutes until the top is firm. Take out of the oven and cover with a teatowel for

a few hours. Spread a sheet of greaseproof paper on a work surface and dust heavily with icing sugar. Turn the roulade out on to this and remove the greaseproof paper lining.

Whip the cream until quite stiff, gradually adding the brandy. Spread the cream over the roulade and dust with icing sugar. Confidently roll the roulade up and dust with icing sugar on the serving dish.

French Peaches

Quick and simple to prepare, this should be served well chilled.

Empty the contents of the cans of peaches, the orange juice and apple slices into a large glass serving bowl, mix lightly then cover with clingfilm and chill in the refrigerator until required.

If liked serve with a crisp biscuit such as Anne Goss's Almond Biscuits (page 47).

2 large cans of white peaches, sliced
½ pint (300 ml) orange juice (fresh or carton)
4 firm red eating apples, cored and sliced

Caramelised Oranges

An easy and refreshing pudding for a buffet party, and it can be prepared the night before.

Thinly peel the rind from two of the oranges, cut it into thin strips, then place in a pan and cover with cold water. Bring to the boil and allow to simmer for 2 minutes until tender then drain off and reserve the water. With a sharp knife cut all the peel and pith off the oranges, then cut the flesh across into about six slices. Reassemble the slices in orange shapes and save all the juice. Stand an orange in each individual serving dish or stand in a large heatproof bowl so they are just touching. Add the cloves.

Measure the sugar into a pan with the water, heat gently until sugar has dissolved then increase heat and boil rapidly for 2 minutes to give a thin syrup. Remove from the heat and add the reserved orange juice and 2 tablespoons of the water in which the rind was boiled. Pour over the oranges, sprinkle with the thin strips of rind, and allow to cool. Cover with clingfilm and chill overnight in the refrigerator before serving.

12 seedless oranges
6 whole cloves
1lb (450g) granulated sugar
¾ pint (450 ml) water

INDIAN
BUFFET

A spread of Indian food is one of the easiest kinds of buffets to do for a large number, and is particularly welcome during the cold winter months.

The Royal Lamb Curry and the Beef Curry were given to me by Khalid Aziz, a specialist in Indian cookery. These are my versions of the recipes, and they are now firm favourites and ideal to serve in an Indian meal. The Royal Lamb Curry has a divine lemony flavour. For a smaller party than the one suggested here, I usually offer two curry dishes and perhaps Tandoori Chicken too, with a choice of the accompaniments which are vital for success.

Something refreshing for pudding after the curry is best. The Indian dessert fruits are always a favourite, or you could perhaps serve Iced Lemon Flummery (page 91) as well as the Mango Icecream (page 121), both of which can be prepared well ahead.

Serve iced water and lager with the meal.

CURRY PARTY FOR 50

2 × **Chicken Curry**
2 × **Royal Lamb Curry**
2 × **Beef Curry**
3 × **Curried Vegetables**

Curry Accompaniments
Rice – use 5½lb (2.5kg)
2 Poppodums per person
4 × Onion and Green Pepper
4 × Banana
6 × Cucumber, Mint and Yoghurt
4 × 16oz (450g) jars of mango chutney and pickles

2 × **Dhal**
2 × **Bombay Salad**

2 × **Indian Dessert Fruits**
2 × **Mango Icecream**
(page 121)

Preparation Hints

The Curries

The great advantage of curries is that they can be made a couple of days beforehand, cooled quickly then kept in the refrigerator and reheated.

Rice

Boil ahead, see recipe.

Poppodums

Best deep-fried then well drained. Do this a day ahead, carefully store in huge plastic bags, and keep in a dry atmosphere.

Onion and Green Pepper

Prepare the day before and cover lightly.

Banana

Slice on the day.

Cucumber, Mint and Yoghurt

Make a couple of hours before needed.

Dhal

Can be made 2 days ahead.

Bombay Salad

Make on the day.

Indian Dessert Fruits

Mix on the day.

Mango Icecream

Make up a couple of weeks ahead.

Chicken Curry

2 inch (5cm) piece of fresh root
    ginger, peeled and chopped
4 fat cloves of garlic, peeled
4 green chillies, seeded
4oz (100g) unsalted cashew nuts
1/2 teaspoon ground cloves
1/2 teaspoon ground cardamom
4 teaspoons ground coriander
1/2 teaspoon ground turmeric
6 fl. oz (175 ml) water
1oz (25g) butter
1 tablespoon sunflower oil
4 onions, chopped
24 chicken thighs, skinned
1 pint (600 ml) natural yoghurt
juice of 1/2 lemon
salt

Chicken thighs are available in most good supermarkets. I usually serve two per person but you might like to add a few more if you have some particularly hungry people amongst your guests.

Put the ginger, garlic, chillies, nuts and all the spices with the water in a processor or blender and reduce to a purée.

    Heat the butter and oil in a pan and fry the onion for about 10 minutes until tender. Add the chicken thighs, spice mixture and yoghurt and mix well. Bring to the boil, cover with a lid and simmer gently for about 45 minutes. Stir in the lemon juice and continue cooking for about 15 minutes or until the chicken is tender. Taste and check seasoning (add some salt if you think it needs it), and serve with plain boiled rice to sop up the sauce.

Tandoori Chicken

12 chicken portions
salt
juice of 2 large lemons
1 1/2 level teaspoons ground
    ginger
4 fat cloves of garlic, crushed
6 green chillies, finely chopped
a few sprigs of fresh mint, finely
    chopped
3/4 pint (450 ml) natural yoghurt
3 level teaspoons chilli seasoning
3 teaspoons ground black pepper
3/4 teaspoon ground nutmeg
3/4 teaspoon garam masala

To serve
shredded lettuce or curly endive

This is one of my favourite dishes when I go to an Indian restaurant to eat. At home, it can be cooked a while before serving, and kept warm on a moderate oven for about 30 minutes or so.

Skin the chicken portions and arrange in a large roasting tin. Mark the chicken with a small sharp knife so that the sauce can penetrate the portions. Sprinkle with salt and lemon juice. Mix all the remaining ingredients together in a bowl and spoon over the chicken portions. Cover with clingfilm and leave to marinate overnight in a cool place.

    To cook the chicken portions, remove the rack from the grill pan and arrange the pieces of chicken in the pan. Grill under a hot grill for about 5 minutes on each side then reduce the heat and cook for a further 10 minutes or so on each side until the chicken is tender.

    To serve, lift the chicken on to a bed of shredded lettuce or curly endive.

Beef Curry

My version of an excellent curry given to me by Khalid Aziz.

Put the meat into a bowl, add the lemon juice, salt and yoghurt, cover with clingfilm and chill in the refrigerator overnight.

Heat the oil in a pan and fry the onion for about 10 minutes until soft then add the turmeric, cumin, paprika, chilli seasoning, ginger and garlic. Cook for about 5 minutes then stir in the meat and yoghurt mixture. Stir well then bring to the boil, cover with a lid and simmer gently for about 45 minutes. Stir in the garam masala, bring back to the simmer and continue to simmer gently for about 1–1½ hours until the meat is tender. Stir from time to time.

4lb (1.8kg) stewing steak
juice of 1 large lemon
salt
2 pints (1.2 litres) natural yoghurt
4 tablespoons sunflower oil
3 large onions, chopped
2 teaspoons ground turmeric
1 teaspoon ground cumin
2 teaspoons paprika
1 teaspoon chilli seasoning
2 inch (5cm) piece of root ginger, peeled and thinly sliced
2 cloves of garlic, crushed
3 teaspoons garam masala

Royal Lamb Curry

The flavour of this lamb dish is absolutely divine. The recipe was given to me by Khalid Aziz, and I have adapted it slightly.

Cut the lamb into 1 inch (2.5cm) cubes. Put in a pan with the stock, cinnamon, bay leaves and the juice and rind from the lemon. Bring to the boil then cover with a lid and simmer gently for about 30 minutes. Lift out the lamb with a slotted spoon and boil the remaining liquid rapidly until reduced by half. Pour this liquid into a processor or blender and add the garlic cloves, cardamoms, cloves and coriander. Blend until smooth.

Heat the oil in a large pan and fry the onion until soft, then add the lamb and fry quickly for a minute. Add the blended mixture, salt, pepper and yoghurt and simmer gently for about 20 minutes. Stir in the cream, almonds and raisins and continue cooking for about 15 minutes until the lamb is tender.

4lb (1.8g) stewing lamb
1 pint (600 ml) good stock
3 inch (7.5cm) stick of cinnamon
3 bay leaves
juice and rind of 1 large lemon
4 fat cloves of garlic, peeled
1 dessertspoon cardamom seeds
1 teaspoon ground cloves
2 tablespoons coriander seeds
4 tablespoons sunflower oil
2 large onions, chopped
salt
freshly ground black pepper
½ pint (300 ml) natural yoghurt
½ pint (300 ml) single cream
4oz (100g) blanched almonds
4oz (100g) raisins

Curried Vegetables

2oz (50g) butter
2 tablespoons sunflower oil
2lb (900g) onions, chopped
2 fat cloves of garlic, crushed
about 1 teaspoon curry powder
2lb (900g) courgettes, sliced
3 aubergines, sliced
4 × 14oz (397g) cans of
  tomatoes
2 teaspoons sugar
salt
freshly ground black pepper

This mixture of vegetables is like a lightly curried ratatouille! Good to serve for a buffet, as it can be prepared well ahead and then kept warm for up to an hour until required. Any longer than this and the vegetables may begin to lose their colour.

Heat the butter and oil in a large pan and fry the onion and the garlic for about 10 minutes until golden brown. Add the curry powder and continue to cook for a further minute, before adding the remaining ingredients. Stir well, bring to the boil then cover with a lid and simmer gently for about 25 minutes until the vegetables are tender. Taste and check seasoning, pour into a warm serving dish and keep warm until required.

Dhal

12oz (350g) green lentils
2 bay leaves
3 tablespoons sunflower oil
2 carrots, chopped
1 large green pepper, chopped
2 onions, chopped
2 fat cloves of garlic, crushed
1 inch (2.5cm) fresh root ginger,
  peeled
1 level teaspoon ground
  cinnamon
1 level teaspoon ground cumin
1 level teaspoon ground coriander
2 × 14oz (397g) cans of
  tomatoes
salt
freshly ground black pepper

Dhal is most often served as an accompaniment to curry but can also be served with pitta bread.

Measure the lentils into a bowl, cover with water and leave to stand overnight. Drain and discard water. Put the lentils in a pan and add sufficient water just to cover. Bring to the boil, add the bay leaves, then cover with a lid and simmer for about 35 minutes until the lentils are tender. Drain and discard the bay leaves.

Heat the oil in a large pan, add the carrot, pepper, onions and garlic and quickly fry for about 10 minutes. Add the pieces of ginger, cinnamon, cumin, coriander, tomatoes and lentils, and simmer gently for about 10 minutes until the carrot is tender. Discard the piece of ginger, then place the mixture in a processor or blender and reduce to a purée (it may be necessary to do this in several batches). Return to the pan, season to taste and reheat to serve.

Curry Accompaniments

These are a vital part of an Indian buffet, and most of them look as well as taste marvellous. Rice and poppodums are the first essentials, then a variety of side dishes or sambols can be served as well.

Rice

I prefer to serve long-grain American rice. Allow 1½–2oz (40–50g) rice per person and cook in plenty of salted water until just tender. Rice is quite easy to reheat: it can either be put in a buttered dish, covered with foil with a few holes in the top and reheated gently in a slow oven, or alternatively it can be plunged into a pan or boiling salted water for about 2 minutes to heat through then drained and served.

Poppodums

These are easily available nowadays in a variety of flavours. They are deep-fat fried, drained well, and then served in a tall pile on the table. Some poppodums can be crisped under the grill.

Onion and Green Pepper

1 large mild Spanish onion, thinly sliced and mixed with finely sliced strips of 2 green peppers. I like to skin the pepper before slicing it. To do this, stand the pepper under a hot grill for about 2 minutes, when the skin will peel off easily.

Banana

Slice 6 bananas and toss in the juice of ½ lemon to prevent discoloration.

Cucumber, Mint and Yoghurt

Stir a ½ cucumber, diced and 2 tablespoons freshly chopped mint into ½ pint (300 ml) natural yoghurt. Season to taste with salt and pepper.

Chutney and Pickles

I always cheat with these and buy them ready-made. Mango chutney, Lime and Brinjal (aubergine) pickles are the best.

Bombay Salad

1 medium red cabbage
1 medium white cabbage
1 large onion, finely chopped
6 tablespoons French dressing
   (page 42)
4oz (100g) Bombay Mix

Bombay Mix is a spicy snack mix bought from health-food shops and ethnic grocers. It contains a wonderful mixture of spiced lentils, split peas, peanuts and crunchy things and is quite delicious scattered over a tossed salad.

Shred the red and white cabbage finely and put into a large serving bowl. Mix the onion and French dressing in a smaller bowl and leave to stand for a couple of hours. Just before serving, pour the onion and French dressing over the cabbage and toss well. Sprinkle the Bombay mix over the top and serve.

Indian Dessert Fruits

1 large can of lychees
8 large seedless oranges

Preferably chill in the refrigerator for at least 12 hours before serving. No need to serve with cream.

Empty the contents of the can of lychees into a serving bowl. With a sharp knife cut all the peel and pith from the oranges and cut into segments, making sure to remove all the pith. Add the orange segments and juice from cutting the oranges to the lychees and mix lightly. Cover with clingfilm and chill in the refrigerator before serving.

MIDDLE EASTERN BUFFET

For this kind of party, you have a wide choice of foods to consider, for the Middle East can be said to include Turkey, Greece, the Lebanon and many of the countries of Arabia and North Africa. It is a good idea to include a well-known dish such as Moussaka for the centrepiece, and surround it with less well-known dishes so that the guests may sample a little of each.

In the summer you could have a barbecue in the garden, serving marinated meat on skewers as kebabs. Marinate chicken or turkey in oil, lemon juice and garlic; beef, lamb or pork in oil, lemon juice and some mixed spice. Serve with pitta breads if you like – or *in* pitta breads – with lots of salads. Tabouleh would go beautifully with kebabs.

Most of the countries in this area do not serve alcohol, of course, but if you're having a Greek buffet, say, you could serve a Retsina or some of the Greek Cypriot wines. Finish the meal with small cups of strong black coffee. If the meal were more North African in flavour, you could serve strong sweet mint tea.

Menu

GREEK BUFFET FOR 12

Taramasalata and Hummus with Pitta Bread

Moussaka

Feta Cheese Salad

Cucumber and Yoghurt Salad

Spiced Potatoes

Baklava

Preparation Hints

A good buffet party, is that only the salads need preparing on the day itself.
It's good for vegetarians too, excluding only the Moussaka.

Taramasalata and Hummus

Make up to 3 days ahead and keep in the fridge. Serve with warmed pitta bread, cut into thick strips to dip. Or serve as you would a pâté, with the pittas or brown bread toast.

Moussaka

Make up to the baking stage 1 or 2 days ahead. Cover and keep in the fridge. Or, if preferred, this could be frozen and then thawed overnight before baking.

The Salads

Prepare ingredients ahead, but only assemble an hour or so before needed.

Spiced Potatoes

Can be prepared in the morning, and then baked for immediate serving.

Baklava

Make a day or two ahead.

Taramasalata

A first-course spread or dip that is good to serve with warmed pitta bread or hot buttered toast.

Remove and discard the skin from the cod's roe. Put into a processor or blender and reduce to a purée.

Soak the bread in the milk, then squeeze out as much milk as possible. Add the bread to the roe and blend again with the garlic. Add the oil a little at a time until all has been absorbed. Stir in the lemon juice and black pepper. Turn into a serving dish and chill well before serving.

1½lb (675g) smoked cod's roe
4 slices of white bread, crusts removed
6 tablespoons milk
2 fat cloves of garlic, crushed
good ½ pint (300 ml) sunflower oil
juice of 1 lemon
freshly ground black pepper

Hummus

A delicious chick-pea spread or dip to serve with warm pitta bread. Tahina paste can be found in delicatessens.

Rinse the chick peas and put in a bowl, cover with cold water and leave to soak overnight. Drain the peas well and put in a pan with enough water to cover them. Bring to the boil and simmer for 2–3 hours until they are very tender, adding salt half way through this time. Drain the peas and reserve the cooking liquid.

Mash the peas to a smooth purée with the garlic and 8 fl. oz (250 ml) of the cooking liquid. This can be done in a processor or blender. Add the lemon juice a little at a time, beating all the time. Add the tahina paste and beat until smooth. Turn into a serving bowl and serve sprinkled with a little cayenne pepper.

1½lb (675g) dried chick peas
salt
6 fat cloves of garlic, crushed
juice of 2 small lemons
1lb (450g) tahina paste
cayenne pepper

Moussaka

3lb (1.4kg) raw lamb, minced
1½lb (675g) onions, chopped
2 fat cloves of garlic, crushed
2½oz (65g) flour
2 × 14oz (397g) cans of
    tomatoes
1 pint (600 ml) good stock
4 tablespoons tomato purée
salt
freshly ground black pepper
1 teaspoon dried mixed herbs
1lb (450g) aubergines

For the sauce
3oz (75g) butter
3oz (75g) flour
1½ pints (900 ml) milk
1 teaspoon ground nutmeg
2 teaspoons made mustard
2 eggs, beaten

For the topping
10oz (275g) well flavoured
    Cheddar cheese, grated
2oz (50g) Parmesan cheese,
    grated

Moussaka is a perfect buffet-party dish. It can be prepared well in advance and then just needs reheating when required. Serve with crisp French bread and a salad.

Heat the oven to 375°F/190°C/Gas Mark 5.

Place the minced lamb in a large pan, and cook over a low heat to let the fat run out. Stir to avoid sticking. When the fat has run freely, add the onions and garlic and increase the heat. Fry for about 20 minutes until the meat has browned and the onions have softened. Add the flour and stir well then add the contents of the cans of tomatoes, the stock, purée, salt, pepper and mixed herbs. Bring to the boil and simmer for 10 minutes. Taste and check seasoning.

Slice the aubergines and blanch in a pan of simmering water for 1 minute. Drain and dry thoroughly on kitchen paper.

For the sauce, melt the butter in a pan, add the flour and cook for a minute, then gradually blend in the milk. Bring to the boil, stirring until thickened. Remove from the heat and stir in some salt and pepper and the nutmeg, mustard and eggs. Mix well.

To assemble the moussaka, first put a layer of the meat mixture into a large ovenproof dish, then cover with half the aubergines. Season, then repeat with the rest of the lamb and aubergines. Pour over the sauce and sprinkle with the cheeses. Bake uncovered in the oven for about 50–60 minutes until the sauce is bubbling and the cheese has melted and is golden brown.

Lamb Kebabs

Choose good quality lean lamb for the kebabs. If liked, they can be cooked on a barbecue for an outdoor party.

Trim any fat from the lamb and cut into small bite size pieces. Arrange the pieces of lamb, tomatoes, pepper and button mushrooms alternately on 12 skewers and lay in a shallow dish so that they are just touching.

Blend the yoghurt, lemon juice, cumin and coriander together in a bowl and add seasoning. Spoon the marinade over the kebabs and leave in a cool place for about 3 hours to marinade. They could be left overnight.

To cook the kebabs, preheat a grill or barbecue and cook for about 10–15 minutes until the lamb is tender. Spoon any remaining marinade from the dish over the kebabs during cooking. Serve straight away with rice and a fresh green salad.

3lb (1.5kg) boned lean lamb
12 firm tomatoes, quartered
4 green peppers, seeded and cut into 1 inch (2.5cm) squares
24 small button mushrooms

For the marinade
½ pint (300 ml) natural yoghurt
juice of 1 lemon
1 teaspoon ground cumin
1 teaspoon ground coriander
salt and black pepper

Spiced Potatoes

Peel and cut the potatoes into ½ inch (1.25cm) cubes. Bring a large pan of salted water to the boil and cook the potatoes for about 5 minutes so that they are still crisp in the centre. Drain well. Heat the oven to 400°F/200°C/Gas Mark 6.

Mix the cumin, fenugreek and mustard seeds together in a bowl. Heat the oil in a large heavy pan until very hot, add the mixed spices and cook for a minute (they will 'pop' when they touch the hot fat), then stir in the sesame seeds and cook for a further 2 minutes. Add the potatoes and fry for 5 minutes, stirring all the time. Season with salt and pepper and stir in the lemon juice. Transfer to a large buttered ovenproof dish and bake uncovered in the oven for about 30 minutes until crisp and golden brown.

3lb (1.4kg) potatoes
3 teaspoons whole cumin seeds
½ teaspoon ground fenugreek
3 teaspoons mustard seeds
6 tablespoons sunflower oil
3 tablespoons sesame seeds
salt
freshly ground black pepper
juice of 1 lemon

Tabouleh

8oz (225g) cracked wheat
6 spring onions, chopped
4 firm tomatoes, skinned, seeded
   and diced
salt
freshly ground black pepper
4 tablespoons freshly chopped
   parsley
2 tablespoons freshly chopped
   mint
6 tablespoons French Dressing
   (page 42)
juice of 1 large lemon

To serve
lettuce leaves
cucumber slices, tomato wedges
   and parsley sprigs

Tabouleh is traditionally served in a bowl lined with cooked vine leaves or raw lettuce leaves (the inner leaves of a Cos lettuce are best, or chinese leaves). The salad is then scooped up in other leaves served in a separate bowl. Cracked wheat (also called bulgur or bulgar wheat) can be bought from most good delicatessens and health good shops.

Measure the cracked wheat into a bowl, cover with water and leave to stand for about 30 minutes. Drain very thoroughly, squeezing out as much liquid as possible. Return to a dry clean bowl and stir in the remaining ingredients. Taste to check seasoning, adding more lemon juice if necessary to give a distinctive lemon flavour to the salad.

Line a serving dish with lettuce leaves, spoon the salad into the centre and decorate with the cucumber, tomato and parsley. Serve with a separate bowl of fresh crisp lettuce leaves.

Serves 12 as part of a buffet

Cucumber and Yoghurt Salad

1 cucumber
¾ pint (450 ml) natural yoghurt
2 fat cloves of garlic, crushed
salt
freshly ground black pepper
3 tablespoons freshly chopped
   mint
a few sprigs of fresh mint, to
   decorate

This is a traditional Turkish dish, and is served a great deal in the Middle East as a starter. Chill the ingredients well then prepare and serve straightaway.

Peel the cucumber and cut the flesh into small cubes. Stir into the yoghurt with the garlic, seasoning and chopped mint. Pour into a serving dish and serve straightaway, decorated with sprigs of fresh mint.

Serves 12 as part of a buffet

Feta Cheese Salad

Feta is a pure white crumbly soft cheese from Greece. It is fairly salty, and it's delicious included in a salad in this way.

Arrange the olives, lettuce leaves, cucumber slices and pepper cubes in a serving bowl. Cut the Feta cheese into triangles and arrange on top. Spoon over the dressing and sprinkle with the freshly chopped parsley.

6oz (175g) fat black olives
1 large crisp lettuce
1½ cucumbers, thickly sliced
1 large green pepper, cubed
12oz (350g) Feta cheese
good ¼ pint (150 ml) French Dressing (page 42)
3 tablespoons freshly chopped parsley

Baklava

Delicious served with whipped cream. Phyllo pastry sheets can be bought in packets in Continental grocers and delicatessens.

Heat the oven to 400°F/200°C/Gas Mark 6. Butter a large swiss roll tin.

Cut the phyllo pastry so that it is roughly the size of the tin. Lay one sheet of pastry in the tin, brush with butter, and continue thus until there are eight layers in the tin. Brush the top layer with butter and sprinkle with the nuts and sugar. Finish with a further eight layers of pastry, still brushing with butter between layers. Brush the top with more butter and cut through to the tin into diamond shapes. Bake in the oven for about 25–30 minutes until a pale golden brown and crispy. Cool.

Meanwhile, make the syrup. Put the water into a pan, add the sugar and the lemon rind, and bring to the boil slowly. Simmer for 15 minutes without a lid. Remove from the heat and add the lemon juice. Remove and discard the peel then pour over the cold baklava. Leave to cool.

12oz (350g) phyllo pastry
6oz (175g) unsalted butter, melted
6oz (175g) walnuts, fairly finely chopped
1½oz (40g) caster sugar

Lemon syrup
8 fl. oz (250 ml) water
12oz (350g) caster sugar
thinly peeled rind and juice of 2 small lemons

TEENAGERS' BUFFET

My teenage sons love to have friends over for supper parties and I find the easiest way to cope with this is to provide the kind of buffet meal that can be left in the oven so that they and their friends can help themselves as and when they are ready. Dishes such as Sausage and Cider Casserole or the Chilli Con Carne are ideal for this as they can be left in the oven with baked potatoes for some time before they begin to spoil.

If it is a particularly nice summer's evening, why not have a barbecue out in the garden? I have included several recipes in this section which can either be cooked outside over charcoal or can equally well be cooked and served indoors. (One advantage of serving the meal outside is that it helps to keep the house tidy!) They can come in afterwards, perhaps, to listen to music, play table tennis or snooker, or simply watch a good video.

For puddings, you could choose anything from any of the other sections that you think would be appreciated. The best idea would probably be to have an icecream bar and make up banana splits etc, with lots of accompaniments (page 105).

Cider Punch would be enjoyed by older teenagers and perhaps for younger ones, Elderflower or Lemon Barley drink. If they like fizzy drinks, then dilute with sparkling water or lemonade.

GARDEN PARTY FOR 12

Pitta Bread 'Sandwiches'

Barbecue Chicken Drumsticks

Beansprout Salad

Barbecue Baked Beans

Pudding of choice

Preparation Hints

Pitta Bread 'Sandwiches'

Prepare the fillings about a couple of hours before the party, and have the breads ready to fill just before serving.

Barbecue Chicken Drumsticks

Cook in advance obviously if serving cold. Prepare in advance and cook before serving hot.

Beansprout Salad

Can be prepared in advance and chilled.

Barbecue Baked Beans

Can be prepared in advance and just heated through before serving.

Menu

KITCHEN SUPPER FOR 12

Mini Pizzas

Sausage and Cider Casserole

Cheesy Baked Potatoes

Pudding of choice

Preparation Hints

Mini Pizzas

These can be prepared well in advance, but cook them at the last moment.

Sausage and Cider Casserole

Prepare in the morning, and cook before serving.

Cheesy Baked Potatoes

Make the fillings in the morning, cook the potatoes in the evening.

Mini Pizzas

These need to be cooked at the last moment, but I leave them laid out on baking trays and then they can be popped in the oven when required.

Heat the butter and oil in a pan and fry the onion for about 10 minutes until tender. Add the contents of the cans of tomatoes with the herbs, seasoning and sugar. Simmer gently for about 15 minutes until thick and pulpy then remove from the heat.

Slice the bread baps in half horizontally and arrange on two large baking trays. Divide the tomato mixture between them and spread out evenly. Sprinkle with the cheese then arrange the anchovy fillets on half of them, and sprinkle the other half with the chopped ham.

When required, heat the oven to 400°F/200°C/Gas Mark 6 and cook the mini pizzas in the oven for about 15–20 minutes until warmed through and the cheese on top has melted and is bubbling.

1oz (25g) butter
1 tablespoon sunflower oil
2 large onions, chopped
2 × 14oz (397g) cans of
    tomatoes
1 teaspoon mixed dried herbs
salt
freshly ground black pepper
2 teaspoons sugar
12 soft bread baps
12oz (350g) well flavoured
    Cheddar cheese, grated
2oz (50g) anchovy fillets,
    drained
4oz (100g) ham, chopped

Spicy Sausage Rolls

These are ideal to serve to teenagers. The stuffing mix spins out the sausagemeat a little further, and makes them that bit more seasoned and herby.

Blend the stuffing mix with the water in a bowl and leave on one side until cold then work in the sausagemeat until evenly blended. Heat the oven to 400°F/200°C/Gas Mark 6.

Roll out the pastry on a lightly floured surface to a large rectangle 11 × 16 inches (27.5 × 40cm), then divide the rectangle into three long equal strips. Divide the sausagemeat into three portions, roll into long sausages, and lay down the middle of the strips of pastry. Brush one side of the pastry with beaten egg then roll up so that the pastry join is underneath the sausage roll. Divide each long sausage into eight sausage rolls.

Arrange on two baking trays, brush the tops with beaten egg, and make two small slits in the top of each with a sharp knife. Bake in the oven for about 35 minutes until well risen and golden brown and the pastry underneath is cooked. Serve warm.

3oz (75g) sage and onion
    stuffing mix
½ pint (300 ml) boiling water
1lb (450g) pork sausagemeat
14oz (400g) packet of frozen
    puff pastry, thawed
1 egg, beaten

Makes about 24 sausage rolls

Pitta Bread 'Sandwiches'

The quantities of each of the fillings below are sufficient to fill two pitta breads
Do be generous with the fillings as this makes the breads all the more delicious
but be sure to have paper napkins at hand, particularly for those with mayon-
naise! Most supermarkets now have both white and wholemeal pitta bread on
their shelves and I usually offer a choice of both. The pitta breads just need
splitting down the side to make an envelope for the filling.

Bacon and Spinach

6oz (175g) streaky bacon,
  chopped
3oz (75g) fresh young spinach
2 good tablespoons thick
  mayonnaise (page 41)

Fry the bacon in a non-stick pan until crispy. Allow to cool. Break the
spinach into small pieces and divide between the two pitta breads. Stir
the bacon into the mayonnaise and spoon into the pitta bread.

Scrambled Egg and Chive

2 eggs, beaten
2 tablespoons milk
salt
freshly ground black pepper
a good knob of butter
2 tablespoons freshly snipped
  chives
shredded iceberg lettuce

Beat the eggs, milk and seasoning together. Heat the butter in a pan
and cook the egg mixture, stirring all the time until just cooked, then
remove from the heat and stir in the chives. Allow to cool. Fill the pitta
bread with a little lettuce then spoon in the scrambled egg.

Prawns in Cocktail Sauce

3 good tablespoons thick
  mayonnaise (page 41)
1 tablespoon tomato ketchup
1 teaspoon Worcestershire sauce
salt
freshly ground black pepper
8oz (225g) peeled prawns
fresh watercress

To make the cocktail sauce, mix all the ingredients except for the
prawns together until thoroughly blended. Taste and check seasoning
then stir in the prawns. Fill the pitta bread with watercress then spoon
in the prawn filling.

Cottage Cheese and Avocado

Fill the pitta bread with a little shredded lettuce. Toss the slices of avocado in the lemon juice to prevent them discolouring, then arrange in the pitta bread. Season the cottage cheese with salt and pepper and spoon into the pitta bread.

a little shredded lettuce
1 avocado, peeled and sliced
juice of ½ lemon
4oz (100g) cottage cheese
salt
freshly ground black pepper

Cheese and Celery

Mix the cheese, celery and yoghurt together in a bowl. Fill the pitta bread with a little lettuce then spoon in the cheese mixture.

6oz (175g) well flavoured
  Cheddar cheese, grated
3 sticks of celery, chopped
3 tablespoons natural yoghurt
a little shredded lettuce

Sausage and Cider Casserole

The children adore this casserole when they have friends round for a party. I just leave it in the oven with some baked potatoes and then they can help themselves.

Heat the oven to 350°F/180°C/Gas Mark 4.

Separate the sausages and fry slowly in a large non-stick pan, in two batches if necessary, until golden brown on all sides. Lift out with a slotted spoon and arrange in the bottom of a large ovenproof casserole dish.

Fry the onion and carrot in the fat remaining in the pan until the onions are beginning to soften. Stir in the flour and cook for a minute, then gradually blend in the cider and the stock. Bring to the boil, stirring until thickened. Add the mushrooms and seasoning and pour over the sausages. Cover with a lid and cook in the oven for about an hour. Serve sprinkled with a little freshly chopped parsley.

3lb (1.4kg) pork chipolata
  sausages
2 medium onions, chopped
12oz (350g) carrots, sliced
2oz (50g) flour
¾ pint (450 ml) cider
¾ pint (450 ml) stock
6oz (175g) button mushrooms,
  sliced
salt
freshly ground black pepper
a little freshly chopped parsley,
  to serve

Chilli Con Carne

1oz (25g) butter
1 tablespoon sunflower oil
4 onions, chopped
4 fat cloves of garlic, crushed
3 green peppers, seeded and cut
    into chunky pieces
2lb (900g) good minced beef
2 × 14oz (397g) cans of
    tomatoes
½ pint (300 ml) good beef stock
2 tablespoons chilli seasoning
2 level teaspoons paprika pepper
salt
2 × 15½oz (439g) cans of red
    kidney beans, drained

This is an excellent dish to serve for a buffet for teenagers. They are quite happy to help themselves and I usually serve lots of crispy French bread with it to sop up the sauce.

Heat the butter and oil in a pan and fry the onion and garlic for about 5 minutes until the onion is tender. Add the green pepper and minced beef and continue to fry for about 10 minutes, stirring continuously. Add the contents of the cans of tomatoes, stock, chilli seasoning, paprika, salt and drained beans. Bring to the boil, cover with a lid and simmer gently for about an hour until the mince is tender. Taste and check seasoning. Serve with crisp French bread.

If made in advance, the chilli can be heated up in the oven at 400°F/200°C/Gas Mark 6 for about 40 minutes or until piping hot.

Barbecue Chicken Drumsticks

24 chicken drumsticks
salt
freshly ground black pepper

For the sauce
2 level tablespoons cornflour
4 tablespoons white wine vinegar
4 tablespoons soy sauce
2 tablespoons Worcestershire
    sauce
3 teaspoons light muscovado
    sugar
8 tablespoons tomato ketchup
6 tablespoons water
2 cloves of garlic, crushed

When serving for a buffet, ensure there are plenty of paper napkins for wiping sticky fingers, or wrap the ends of the drumsticks in foil so they can be easily picked up and eaten in the fingers. They can be cooked over charcoal or the barbecue, and they will need to be basted often with the sauce.

Heat the oven to 350°F/180°C/Gas Mark 4.

Season the chicken drumsticks with salt and pepper and arrange in a large roasting tin. Blend all the ingredients for the sauce together in a pan and bring to the boil, stirring until thickened. Pour over the drumsticks and turn the drumsticks over in the sauce so they are evenly coated. Cover with foil and cook in the oven for 30 minutes then remove the foil, baste the drumsticks and return to the oven for about a further 15 minutes until tender. Serve hot or cold.

American Hashed Beef

A very delicious savoury mince which is good to cook in large quantities for a party and then serve with baked potatoes and salad. A real treat and something they can make for themselves.

Place the minced beef in a large pan and cook gently until the fat begins to run out, then increase the heat. Add the onion and continue to cook for about 10 minutes until the meat has browned and the onion has softened. Stir in the remaining ingredients. Bring to the boil, cover with a lid and simmer gently for about 40 minutes or until the meat is tender, stirring from time to time. Taste to check seasoning then serve piping hot.

2½lb (1.25kg) lean minced beef
3 large onions, chopped
10½oz (300g) can of condensed vegetable soup
10½oz (300g) can of condensed tomato soup
11oz (335g) can of sweetcorn, drained
2 × 14oz (397g) cans of tomatoes
salt
freshly ground black pepper
1 tablespoon Worcestershire sauce

Cheesy Baked Potatoes

Everyone loves crispy baked potatoes and they are a good way of filling hungry young people up. Serve the filling separately so they can just help themselves.

Heat the oven to 400°F/200°C/Gas Mark 6. Scrub the potatoes well, cut in half and arrange on a large baking tray, cut side upwards. Brush evenly with oil, score the tops with a sharp knife and sprinkle with the cheese. Bake in the oven for about 1½ hours until tender (the cooking time will vary with the size of the potatoes). Serve with a choice of the following toppings.

12 large potatoes
a little sunflower oil
6oz (175g) well flavoured Cheddar cheese, grated

Tomato and Bacon

Cook the bacon in a non-stick pan until the fat begins to run out then increase the heat, stir in the onion, and continue to cook until the bacon is crispy and the onion is tender. Add the contents of the can of tomatoes, salt, pepper and sugar, and cook for about 10 minutes until thick and pulpy. Taste and check seasoning and serve hot with the potatoes.

8oz (225g) streaky bacon, chopped
1 onion, chopped
14oz (397g) can of tomatoes
salt
freshly ground black pepper
1 teaspoon sugar

Soured Cream and Onion

1 bunch of spring onions,
    chopped
½ pint (300 ml) soured cream

Stir the onions into the cream and serve in a bowl with the potatoes.

Curry Sauce

½ pint (300 ml) good thick
    mayonnaise (page 41)
2 tablespoons tomato purée
3 tablespoons mango chutney,
    chopped
juice of ½ lemon
1 teaspoon curry powder
salt
freshly ground black pepper

Blend all the ingredients together and serve in a bowl with the potatoes.

Barbecue Baked Beans

1oz (25g) butter
2 tablespoons sunflower oil
2 large onions, chopped
2 × 15oz (375g) cans of baked
    beans in tomato sauce
4oz (100g) dark muscovado
    sugar
4 tablespoons Worcestershire
    sauce
freshly ground black pepper
2 teaspoons Dijon mustard
6 tablespoons tomato ketchup

For variety add a little bacon with the onion when frying or a little chopped celery or chopped green pepper.

Heat the butter and oil in a pan and fry the onion for about 10 minutes until tender. Add the remaining ingredients to the pan, mix well and heat through. Simmer gently for about 10 minutes so the sugar dissolves and the flavours can develop.

Serve with barbecued food such as sausages, beefburgers and chicken drumsticks.

Beansprout Salad

Very popular with teenagers and very healthy as well! All the ingredients just need tossing together.

Measure all the ingredients into a large bowl and toss well. Cover with clingfilm and chill in the refrigerator until required. Turn into a serving bowl to serve.

8oz (225g) beansprouts
1lb (450g) tomatoes, quartered
½ cucumber, diced
6 spring onions, chopped
6 tablespoons French Dressing
    (page 42)

Hot Barbecue Sauce

Good to serve with most barbecued food such as chops, sausages and beef-burgers.

Heat the butter in a pan and fry the onion, celery and garlic for about 10 minutes until soft. Stir in the remaining ingredients and bring to the boil. Simmer gently for about 15 minutes then remove the bay leaf and serve.

1oz (25g) butter
1 small onion, very finely
    chopped
1 stick of celery, very finely
    chopped
1 fat clove of garlic, crushed
2 tablespoons dry mustard
    powder
2 tablespoons light muscovado
    sugar
½ teaspoon Tabasco
14oz (397g) can of tomatoes
2 tablespoons Worcestershire
    sauce
juice of 2 lemons
4 tablespoons cider or white wine
    vinegar
1 bay leaf

PARTY DRINKS

Deciding on how much drink to buy for a party is often difficult. It really depends on the length of the party and the age of the guests: I find the young and the very old drink less! For a longish evening drinking wine only, allow at least three-quarters of a bottle per head.

Choosing what to serve is a very personal matter, depending upon what you like and what you can afford. For larger numbers for a 'non-theme' buffet party, I find it best to start with sherry or Bucks Fizz (we mix fresh orange juice with chilled sparkling wine, not champagne, for this). Or, for a change, particularly in summer, I like to serve Kir or Kir Royale. If you know that the men will enjoy beer then serve this as well. You know your guests best and what they are likely to prefer to drink. Have pre-mixed drinks if possible, but don't try to serve three kinds if you are entertaining over twelve people. You'll go mad, and they'll go dry!

If you are serving one of my 'national' buffets, then try to match a pre-meal drink with the specific country: a good cocktail for an American meal, a Pastis or Pernod before a French meal, etc. I offer a few suggestions in the introductions to each section.

With the meal, offer white or red wine, and once again try to match the country of origin of the wine to the theme of your buffet. Have a back-up of chilled soft drinks for later in the evening: Perrier and other mineral waters should be available too.

Many wine merchants sell drinks on a sale or return basis. Most suppliers loan glasses free of charge, and you pay for any breakages. (They expect you to return them clean.) Over-order glasses rather than under-order, as glasses tend to get mislaid during the party.

Bucks Fizz

Mix in jugs just before it is needed. Ideally use either reconstituted frozen orange juice or fresh orange juice in cartons from the supermarket.

Makes about 14 glasses

2 bottles dry sparkling wine or champagne, very well chilled
1 pint (600 ml) fresh orange juice, chilled

Kir

Mix in jugs before needed.

Makes about 12 glasses

2 bottles chilled dry white wine
¼ pint (150 ml) Cassis

Kir Royale

As above but use chilled sparkling wine. (To be correct, it should be champagne!)

Gluhwein

A delicious warming mulled wine to serve with savouries before a buffet at winter parties. The wine can be kept warm over a low heat, in a vacuum flask or in a slow cooker if you have one.

Thinly peel the zest from the lemons. Cut a few slices for garnish and then squeeze the remaining fruit to extract all the juice. Put the lemon zest, juice, wine, water, cloves and cinnamon in a large saucepan. Put on the lid, bring the mixture to just below simmering point and leave at this temperature for an hour or more. Remove the lemon rind, cloves and cinnamon and add sugar to taste. Add the brandy just before serving to get a more potent drink. Serve hot with slices of lemon floating on top.

Makes about 20 glasses

4 lemons
2 bottles of inexpensive red wine
2 pints (1.2 litres) water
16 cloves
2 sticks of cinnamon
4–8oz (100g–200g) caster sugar
8 tablespoons cheap brandy or sherry

Sangria

4 pints (2.25 litres) sweet cider
2 bottles of inexpensive red wine
1 glass of brandy
3oz (75g) caster sugar
1 large lemon, sliced
2 oranges, sliced
2 eating apples, cored and sliced
1 tray of ice cubes

Quick and easy to prepare, it should be served really well chilled, so is best for a summer party.

Chill the cider and wine in the refrigerator overnight.
    To serve, mix all the ingredients together in a large mixing bowl and serve straightaway in wine glasses.

Makes 12 generous glasses

Cider Punch

1 pint (600 ml) tonic water
1 pint (600 ml) cider
6¼oz (175g) carton of frozen
    concentrated orange juice
1 tray of ice cubes
a few sprigs of fresh mint
1 orange, sliced

This, too, is a delicious drink to serve on a hot day.

Chill the tonic and cider overnight in the refrigerator.
    To serve, make the orange juice up to a pint (600 ml) with cold water and add the tonic water, cider and ice cubes. Mix well and serve in glasses with sprigs of mint and a slice of orange.

Makes about 12 glasses

Sparkling Cider Cup

1 bottle dry white wine
1 bottle Pomagne
1 orange, sliced
a few sprigs of fresh mint

A very refreshing drink, good to serve in the summer. If you prefer a sweeter drink then use a sweet white wine rather than a dry one. To make it less alcoholic, add a bottle of lemonade! It goes further too.

Thoroughly chill the wine and Pomagne. Blend the two together just before serving and decorate with slices of fresh orange and a few sprigs of mint.

Makes about 12 glasses

Lemon Barley Water

This is wonderfully refreshing on a hot day. Serve really well chilled.

Measure the pearl barley into a pan, cover with cold water and bring to the boil. Reduce the heat and simmer for 5 minutes then drain and discard the cooking water. Turn the barley into a large bowl. Peel the lemons thinly and add the peel to the bowl with the sugar and boiling water. Leave overnight.

The next day, strain and stir in the lemon juice. Pour into a large jug and chill in the refrigerator until required. Serve with ice cubes and sprigs of fresh mint.

Makes about 12 glasses

12oz (350g) pearl barley
4 large lemons
8oz (225g) granulated sugar
5 pints (2.75 litres) boiling water

To serve
ice cubes
sprigs of fresh mint

Elderflower Syrup

Good to make around the beginning of July when the elderberry bushes are a mass of flowers.

Measure the sugar and boiling water into a large bowl and stir until sugar has dissolved. Peel the lemons and grapefruit thinly and add the pieces of peel to the sugar syrup with the juices from the lemons and grapefruit, the citric acid and elderflower heads. Cover with clingfilm and leave to stand overnight.

Strain off the peel and flowerheads and bottle the syrup. Store in the refrigerator for up to a month, or freeze for up to a year in polythene containers or as ice cubes. To serve dilute to taste with iced water.

1½lb (675g) granulated sugar
2 pints (1.2 litres) boiling water
2 small lemons
1 grapefruit
1oz (25g) citric acid
6 large elderflower heads with stalks trimmed

INDEX

184

ROBYN WILSON

FISH

The complete A–Z of over a hundred irresistible fish and shellfish, covering everything you need to know about buying, preparing and cooking this most versatile and appetizing food – for beginner and expert alike.

FISH for your health
– Halve your chances of a heart attack
– Increase your resistance to arthritis, migraine headaches, multiple sclerosis, eczema, breast cancer and high blood pressure
– Increase your brain power

FISH for your figure
– Lose weight with low calorie fish
– Keep your skin supple, your eyes bright and your hair shiny
– Reduce the cholesterol level in your diet

FISH for your sex life
– Enhance your potency, fertility and libido

FISH – the ultimate guide to a new lifestyle of health and fitness.

0 7474 0037 7   NON-FICTION   £2.50

A selection of bestsellers from Sphere

FICTION

THE LEGACY OF HEOROT	Niven/Pournelle/Barnes	£3.50 ☐
THE PHYSICIAN	Noah Gordon	£3.99 ☐
INFIDELITIES	Freda Bright	£3.99 ☐
THE GREAT ALONE	Janet Dailey	£3.99 ☐
THE PANIC OF '89	Paul Erdman	£3.50 ☐

FILM AND TV TIE-IN

BLACK FOREST CLINIC	Peter Heim	£2.99 ☐
INTIMATE CONTACT	Jacqueline Osborne	£2.50 ☐
BEST OF BRITISH	Maurice Sellar	£8.95 ☐
SEX WITH PAULA YATES	Paula Yates	£2.95 ☐
RAW DEAL	Walter Wager	£2.50 ☐

NON-FICTION

FISH	Robyn Wilson	£2.50 ☐
THE SACRED VIRGIN AND THE HOLY WHORE	Anthony Harris	£3.50 ☐
THE DARKNESS IS LIGHT ENOUGH	Chris Ferris	£4.50 ☐
TREVOR HOWARD: A GENTLEMAN AND A PLAYER	Vivienne Knight	£3.50 ☐
INVISIBLE ARMIES	Stephen Segaller	£4.99 ☐

All Sphere books are available at your local bookshop or newsagent, or can be ordered direct from the publisher. Just tick the titles you want and fill in the form below.

Name _____

Address _____

_____

Write to Sphere Books, Cash Sales Department, P.O. Box 11, Falmouth, Cornwall TR10 9EN

Please enclose a cheque or postal order to the value of the cover price plus:

UK: 60p for the first book, 25p for the second book and 15p for each additional book ordered to a maximum charge of £1.90.

OVERSEAS & EIRE: £1.25 for the first book, 75p for the second book and 28p for each subsequent title ordered.

BFPO: 60p for the first book, 25p for the second book plus 15p per copy for the next 7 books, thereafter 9p per book.

Sphere Books reserve the right to show new retail prices on covers which may differ from those previously advertised in the text elsewhere, and to increase postal rates in accordance with the P.O.